PSYCHOLOGY RESEARCH PROGRESS

# CHILD AND SCHOOL PSYCHOLOGY

# PSYCHOLOGY RESEARCH PROGRESS

Additional books in this series can be found on Nova's website under the Series tab.

Additional E-books in this series can be found on Nova's website under the E-books tab.

PSYCHOLOGY RESEARCH PROGRESS

# CHILD AND SCHOOL PSYCHOLOGY

MEREDITH HAINES
AND
ALLISON PEARCE
EDITORS

Nova Science Publishers, Inc.
*New York*

For permission to use material from this book please contact us:
Telephone 631-231-7269; Fax 631-231-8175
Web Site: http://www.novapublishers.com

## NOTICE TO THE READER



## Library of Congress Cataloging-in-Publication Data

Child and school psychology / editors, Meredith Haines and Allison Pearce.
p. cm.
Includes index.
ISBN 978-1-61470-801-8 (hardcover)
1. School psychology. 2. Educational psychology. 3. School children--Mental health services. I. Haines, Meredith. II. Pearce, Allison.
LB1027.55.C44 2011
370.15--dc23
2011026242

*Published by Nova Science Publishers, Inc. †New York*

# Contents

# PREFACE

This book gathers research from across the globe in the study of child and school psychology. Topics discussed include the current state of schools in the U.S. today and student performance; mental health providers and children with medical conditions in school; the academic and social-emotional benefits of including mindfulness based stress reduction in K-12 education; multi-disciplinary teamwork in special education schools and speech and hearing services in urban special education schools in South Africa.

Chapter 1 – Although the current state of schools in the United States is concerning to many, it is evident that schools continue to play a strong role in the lives of our children and have the potential to set the tone for our children's futures. Nonetheless, schools are facing numerous challenges. In particular, schools are facing situations in which they do not have sufficient financial resources to provide all the materials and services that are needed by their students, they face limitations in their ability to hire high quality teachers, they have low expectations for student performance (e.g., Eastin, 2008), and they over-emphasize annual achievement test scores to the detriment of students' actual learning and problem solving (in conjunction with the accountability that is now in place). Although some may think that children may be somewhat removed from these difficulties, research suggests that children are experiencing some effects. For example, only 29 percent of students in the Sixth through Twelfth Grades reported that their schools provided caring and encouraging environments (DeAngelis, 2010). Such perceptions may be affecting boys more than girls, as boys are less likely to remain engaged in their academic settings, less likely to keep pace academically with their female counterparts, and less likely to attend college (Chamberlin, 2008). Boys also are more likely to be rated as having externalizing behavior problems and attentional difficulties relative to their female counterparts (Rescorla, Achenbach, Ginzburg, et al., 2007; Rescorla, Achenbach, Ivanova, et al., 2007), although some of these ratings may be a function of teachers' perceptions of students' behavior. Rather than continue with the current status quo, some researchers are suggesting that schools should take a more holistic approach to educating our children. In such an approach, school services would be integrated with other community-based resources and services (Power, DuPaul, Shapiro, and Kazak, 2003), and schools would attend to children's social-emotional needs as well as the more typically addressed academic achievement needs. Given the importance of understanding the challenges being faced by schools today as well as how these concerns may be affecting our children, these concerns as well as possible solutions will be explored in this chapter.

Chapter 2 – Before most children enter school, his/her primary experience with language is in the oral mode (Gambrell, 2004; Nation and Snowling, 2004). Once the child arrives at school, language becomes more abstract, as it becomes the vehicle of learning (Nelson, 1985). Without adequate language skills, learning in a classroom setting becomes difficult. Westby (1985) explains that on the oral-to-literate continuum, school activities are at the extreme literate end of the spectrum. This means the child is required to comprehend and convey information that is disconnected from his/her own experience. Abadiano and Turner (2005, pp. 60) state, "To become a skilled reader, children need a rich language and conceptual knowledge base, a broad and deep vocabulary, and verbal reasoning abilities to understand messages that are conveyed through print." It is evident from this statement that language development must precede literacy development. Children must be proficient in oral language before they can learn to read and write (Catts and Fey, 1999; Roth, Speece, and Cooper, 2002). It should be noted that children with language impairments are at high risk for literacy disabilities (Lewis, O'Donnell, Freebairn, and Taylor, 1998). Abadiano and Turner (2005), also highlight the importance of preschool attendance as a predictor of literacy success later in the school career.

Chapter 3 – This chapter reviews the roles for mental health professionals working with children who have chronic medical conditions in schools. Mental health professionals have several roles in assisting children with chronic illnesses. For example, they are able network with teachers and school nurses to develop care plans to ensure that teachers understand and meet the special needs of children with medical conditions. Developing written, individualized care plans is a way to ensure that the school and parents have a mutual understanding and acceptance of the best methods for meeting the child's needs to promote academic as well as social and emotional development. A section on health literacy reviews the importance of providing medical information in ways that teachers and children understand. Suggestions for working with children are provided from a noncategorical perspective, in that these ideas are helpful irrespective of the type of illness that the child is facing. Also, we present ideas for helping children who have cancer and cerebral palsy, as our examples of two specific illnesses. Ideas for future research are presented at the close of this chapter. Participatory research and single case designs are practical research designs for use in the schools, and these methods will allow professionals to focus on needs of the child within an ecological perspective.

Chapter 4 – Schools offer a variety of educational programs, such as Drivers' Ed and Sex Ed, to promote youth's responsible behavior, protect their health, and increase their ability to learn. Given the protective benefits of such educational efforts, and the pervasive stresses children and adolescents face on a daily basis, schools must also educate youth about how to cope effectively with psychological stress. Stress has a major influence on child and adolescent psychology, and contributes to depression, anxiety, eating disorders, addictions, suicide and other psychological and health ailments. Stress also has a negative impact on learning. Therefore, it is important that stress reduction be incorporated into school-based education to promote learning, pro-social behavior, and well-being. This chapter discusses the concept of stress education (Stress Ed), a mindfulness based stress reduction curriculum, and how such a curriculum might minimize student distress, enhance learning, and increase pro-social behavior. We first describe the prevalence of child and adolescent stress-related disorders and the impact of these disorders on academic learning, healthy social development, and risk taking behaviors. Then, we describe the essential components of mindfulness- based stress reduction (MBSR) programs as a foundation for creating Stress Ed curricula. Next, we review the preliminary data regarding the benefits of offering MBSR and related mindfulness programs to K-12 students. Finally, we discuss the current challenges to school-based Stress Ed and offer potential solutions.

Chapter 5 – In recent decades both researchers and professionals agree that inter-disciplinary team collaboration has become a particularly important component of work planning and implementation in inclusive and special education schools. Collaboration inter-disciplinary teamwork is a vibrant realm of social processes and complex framework of activity. This study examines and analyzes how collaborative Collaboration inter-disciplinary teamwork in a special education school takes place in everyday life. This is ethnographic case study which examines the activities of 65 members of an inter-disciplinary team: educators, therapist and physicians working in collaboration in a special education school. Data was gathered through observations (formal and informal) of inter-disciplinary team meetings, individual interviews and document collection during one year of research. Analysis of the data indicates that Collaboration is based on three components: contents, structures and processes. This component is examined with respect to Collaboration objectives. The uniqueness of this research lies in the understanding and presentation of the complexity of the functioning of an multi -disciplinary team in daily life. Data findings may be utilized as a conceptual platform for research and professionals in the field in examining additional question and may also serve as the basis for designing applies tools for working with multi-disciplinary team in education in general and in special education in particular.

Chapter 6 – In South Africa there is an increased demand of therapy services in schools for learners with special education needs (LSEN) as well as a generalised lack of funding and professionals to provide for these services. According to the Executive Objective Summary, KwaZulu-Natal (KZN) as a province is facing similar challenges to those of the country as a whole. The priority areas for social, economic and demographic development include rural development, urban renewal, economic and employment growth, poverty reduction and human resource development (Statistics South Africa, Census 2001). With regards to the role of Speech Language Pathologists (SLPs) and Audiologists in schools for learners with special education needs (LSEN), there is currently no research in the KwaZulu-Natal (KZN) province that has investigated the professional role of the SLP and audiologist, thus it was crucial to conduct the current study. The services provided in terms of demographical information, availability of services, case load information, resources available and needed, as well as intervention and treatment systems that are in place were also described and explored.

In: Child and School Psychology
Editors: M. Haines et al., pp. 1-50
ISBN: 978-1-61470-801-8


*Chapter 1*

# ARE SCHOOLS FAILING OUR CHILDREN?

***Kimberly Renk**, Brea-Anne Lauer, Meagan McSwiggan, Jayme Puff, Rebecca Weaver, Melissa Middleton, Rachel White, and Amanda Lowell***
University of Central Florida, US

## ABSTRACT

Although the current state of schools in the United States is concerning to many, it is evident that schools continue to play a strong role in the lives of our children and have the potential to set the tone for our children's futures. Nonetheless, schools are facing numerous challenges. In particular, schools are facing situations in which they do not have sufficient financial resources to provide all the materials and services that are needed by their students, they face limitations in their ability to hire high quality teachers, they have low expectations for student performance (e.g., Eastin, 2008), and they over-emphasize annual achievement test scores to the detriment of students' actual learning and problem solving (in conjunction with the accountability that is now in place).

---

* This manuscript is dedicated to K.R.'s son, in response to his initial experience in Kindergarten. Luckily, a new school made things right for him, and this chapter made things right for his Mom. Please address correspondence to: Kimberly Renk, Ph.D., University of Central Florida, Department of Psychology, P.O. Box 161390, Orlando, Florida 32816. E-mail: Kimberly.Renk@ucf.edu

Although some may think that children may be somewhat removed from these difficulties, research suggests that children are experiencing some effects. For example, only 29 percent of students in the Sixth through Twelfth Grades reported that their schools provided caring and encouraging environments (DeAngelis, 2010). Such perceptions may be affecting boys more than girls, as boys are less likely to remain engaged in their academic settings, less likely to keep pace academically with their female counterparts, and less likely to attend college (Chamberlin, 2008). Boys also are more likely to be rated as having externalizing behavior problems and attentional difficulties relative to their female counterparts (Rescorla, Achenbach, Ginzburg, et al., 2007; Rescorla, Achenbach, Ivanova, et al., 2007), although some of these ratings may be a function of teachers' perceptions of students' behavior.

Rather than continue with the current status quo, some researchers are suggesting that schools should take a more holistic approach to educating our children. In such an approach, school services would be integrated with other community-based resources and services (Power, DuPaul, Shapiro, and Kazak, 2003), and schools would attend to children's social-emotional needs as well as the more typically addressed academic achievement needs. Given the importance of understanding the challenges being faced by schools today as well as how these concerns may be affecting our children, these concerns as well as possible solutions will be explored in this chapter.

It is clear that schools play an important role in the lives of children today. Some would argue, however, that the United States should focus on education with greater intensity. This argument would be supported by the facts that the global economy is fostering a need for higher education and that higher performing countries have a higher set of standards for secondary education than those that exist in the United States (Eastin, 2008). Although national standards are needed, the No Child Left Behind (NCLB) law calls for states to develop their own standards (Eastin, 2008). Such legislation has a great impact on the operation of our schools and the content areas that are taught to our children. For example, although the United States is falling behind considerably in science, NCLB actually encourages less instruction in science and writing. As a result, these topics now are assessed less frequently than skills in other academic domains (e.g., reading and math; Eastin, 2008).

Even with the importance of schools, schools are facing a number of challenges, including a lack of adequate financial resources, low expectations for student performance, and limits on faculty (e.g., not enough teachers, lack of time; Eastin, 2008). Further, many suggest that schools in the United States fail to foster adaptive mental health and strong connections with other individuals (e.g., peers, adults). For example, DeAngelis (2010) reports that only 29 percent of students in the Sixth through Twelfth Grades report that their schools provide caring and encouraging environments. Such difficulties may manifest themselves more readily for boys relative to girls and through bullying interactions in today's school environments. As a result, this chapter plans to explore some of the issues that schools are facing as well as some of the difficulties that need to be addressed in an effort to illuminate the kinds of characteristics that ideal school environments should possess.

## THE ROLE OF SCHOOLS

When the role of schools in children's lives is examined, it is clear that schools are vital to many developments throughout the childhood and adolescent years. Most obviously, schools play a role in fostering children's acquisition of academic information and children's ultimate academic achievement. Nonetheless, schools also play a role in children's typical development and the skills that children must acquire to function socially with their peers and other individuals. These roles will be examined first.

### Academic Achievement

A primary goal for schools is fostering children's academic achievement (Merrow, 2001). Academic achievement can be defined as the skills that children learn through direct intervention or instruction across different academic domains (Stetson, Stetson, and Sattler, 2001). The overarching aim of promoting the academic achievement of children and adolescents is to ensure their success as they transition into the workforce or college settings. Given this ultimate goal of academic achievement, it is clearly an important aspect of children's development and can serve as a protective factor in children's lives. In addition, it is a complex construct that is influenced by a number of ontogenic, familial, and environmental variables. For example, research suggests that an achievement disparity exists across children of different ethnicities and socioeconomic statuses (Jencks and Phillips, 1998). The purpose of this section is to highlight correlates of academic achievement, discuss exceptionalities in achievement as well as how schools address these exceptionalities, and briefly describe popular methods of measuring academic achievement.

*Correlates of Academic Achievement.* Children's academic achievement can be considered a protective factor, as it fosters the promotion of resiliency (Jackson, 1994), positive peer relationships (Meijs, Cillessen, Scholte, Segers, and Spijkerman, 2010; Newcomb, Bukowski, Pattee, 1993), healthy adult functioning (Furnee, Groot, and van den Brink, 2008; Jackson, 1994), and an increased likelihood of children's ultimate transition into college or the workforce (Tanner, 2003). In addition, students who are unsuccessful in school are more likely to experience emotional and behavioral difficulties (Schwartz, Hopmeyer Gorman, Duong, and Nakamoto, 2008) and school dropout (Tanner, 2003). Similarly, there are a number of factors that are thought to influence children's academic achievement. For example, familial characteristics (Byrnes, 2003; Magnuson, 2007; Mandara, Varner, Greene, and Richman, 2009), personality characteristics (for more information, see Nolfte and Robins, 2007, and Trautwein, Ludtke, Roberts, Schnyder, and Niggli, 2009), and emotional and behavioral difficulties (Ansary and Luthar, 2009; Frick et al., 1991; Hinshaw, 1992; Reinke, Herman, Petras, and Ialongo, 2008) are each examples of variables that are associated with children's success or failure in academic achievement.

Given the reciprocal relationships between children's academic achievement and their functioning, it becomes obvious that relationships involving academic achievement are often complex and dependent on a number of variables. For example, research clearly indicates that family characteristics, such as parents' socioeconomic status and education levels, are predictive of children's academic achievement (Lee and Burkam, 2002). Magnuson (2007) examines more closely mothers' education levels and children's academic achievement and reports that mothers' *age* is a significant predictor of children's academic success when mothers receive more schooling. In addition, Magnuson (2007) reports that mothers' receipt of additional schooling is related to improvements in children's reading scores more so than in their math scores.

A second example of the complex nature of children's academic achievement is discussed in Hinshaw's (1992) examination of the relationship between children's externalizing problems and academic achievement. Hinshaw (1992) describes a number of hypotheses regarding causal models of children's externalizing problems and academic achievement. For example, it may be that underachievement is a precursor to externalizing problems, that externalizing problems are precursors to underachievement, that the externalizing problems and underachievement relationship is bidirectional, or that other variables (e.g., environmental and individual characteristics) lead to problems in both areas. Hinshaw (1992) further indicates that, although research has sought to better understand the mechanisms underlying the relationships between children's externalizing problems and academic achievement, a clear picture is not yet available and may not be achieved easily given the number of other related variables that must be considered.

Thus, it is increasingly important that schools, teachers, and parents be aware of the importance of academic achievement throughout the lifespan and consider closely the many factors that may foster and hinder children from succeeding academically. Such an understanding becomes increasingly important (and complex) as children from different ethnicities and socio-economic status levels are considered.

*Disparities in Achievement.* Research suggests that academic success is not necessarily equal across children from different ethnic backgrounds (for more information, see Jencks and Phillips, 1998). Such disparities in achievement are complex and have been explained by a number of factors, such as family characteristics across generations, socioeconomic status, parents' level of education, and parenting styles or practices (Bradley et al., 1989; Brooks-Gunn, Klebanov, Smith, Duncan, and Lee, 2003; Byrnes, 2003; Mandara et al., 2009). For example, Mandara and colleagues' (2009) intergenerational study of African American and European American families examines each of these familial characteristics. This study provides strong evidence that the effects of parenting practices and socioeconomic status are passed down across the generations and subsequently are related to children's current academic achievement. In particular, Mandara and colleagues (2009) describe a cycle in which European American's socioeconomic advantage influences parenting practices that promote academic excellence and subsequently influence children's ability to grow up and obtain career and financial success. In turn, these individuals parent in a way that promotes the same types of outcomes in their children, the next generation. In contrast, in the context of differential socioeconomic status, the opposite is sometimes true for African American children, as the families of African American children have access to fewer socioeconomic resources (Mandara et al., 2009).

Such research highlights the importance of schools and teachers recognizing the academic achievement gap that may be evident across children from different socioeconomic backgrounds. Schools can address gaps in academic achievement in a number of ways, including taking steps to be aware of cultural and ethnic differences and to avoid penalizing children academically for differences in learning (Council for Exceptional Children, 2003; Villegas and Lucas, 2007); working closely with families to encourage involvement and support for the academic process, especially if disabilities are present (Pullen, 2004); and implementing effective teaching strategies for children from all types of backgrounds (Banks and Banks, 2007).

*Exceptionalities Across Students.* Children's academic achievement also is influenced by intellectual exceptionalities (e.g., mental retardation, giftedness) and learning disabilities. Given that class curricula are designed typically for students whose intelligence is within the average range, special considerations are needed for those whose intelligence is at extreme ends of the continuum (i.e., either significantly higher or lower than average). Such considerations are particularly important given the high correlation between intelligence and academic achievement. For example, children who struggle with an intellectual disability may benefit from having an educational curriculum that includes a combination of academics and functional skills (Drew and Hardman, 2004), systematic instruction (e.g., use of prompts, consequences for performance, strategies for the transfer of stimulus control; Davis and Cuvo, 1997), and a behavioral intervention plan (Horner, Albin, Sprague, and Todd, 2000).

On the opposite end of the spectrum are children who are identified as gifted. Giftedness refers to intellectual superiority (i.e., those whose intelligence falls in the upper two percent of the population), creativity, and motivation (Hallahan, Kauffman, and Pullen, 2009). These children also have educational needs that differ from their peers and would benefit from having an advanced curriculum (see VanTassel-Baska and Stambaugh, 2006), unique and creative instructional strategies catered toward their manner of learning (see Davis and Rimm, 2004), and classroom placement with children who have similarly developed abilities (see Callahan, 2000). Different schools provide these types of services in a variety of ways, ranging from advanced curricula, resource rooms, mentor programs, special classes, and rapid advancement of students through grade levels (Hallahan et al., 2009).

Still other children may have intelligence and academic achievement scores that differ significantly, resulting in the diagnosis of a learning disability (IDEA, 2004). Students who have learning disabilities require different accommodations to ensure their academic success. A number of educational considerations have been suggested for children with learning disabilities (for a thorough review, see Hallahan et al., 2009), including cognitive training (e.g., self instruction, self-monitoring, scaffolded instruction, and reciprocal teaching; Hallahan, Lloyd, Kauffman, Weiss, and

Martinez, 2005), use of graphic organizers or mnemonics (e.g., content enhancement; Gajria, Jitendra, Sood, and Sacks, 2007), direct instruction by teachers (Ellis and Fouts, 1997), and peer tutoring (Kourea, Cartledge, and Musti-Rao, 2007). Given the many different needs of these children and those with other disabilities or extraordinary academic achievement not described here, schools face ongoing challenges of creating effective curricula while accommodating children's needs and allocating the resources that are needed to make learning and achievement possible for all children.

*Measuring Achievement.* When measuring children's academic achievement, many different achievement tests are available. For example, a number of popular comprehensive achievement tests that evaluate children's strengths and weaknesses across different areas of achievement exist. These tests can assist in the identification of children's exceptionalities, including giftedness and learning disabilities. The *Woodcock-Johnson Test of Achievement-Third Edition* (WJ-III; Woodcock, McGrew, and Mather, 2001), the *Wechsler Individual Achievement Test-III* (WIAT-III; Burns, 2010), and the *Kaufman Tests of Educational Achievement- Second Edition* (KTEA-II; Kaufman and Kaufman, 2004) are premier examples of such tests. Each of these tests are designed to measure three or more subject areas (e.g., reading, written language, mathematics) and to assess for skills requiring both higher and lower levels of achievement (Stetson et al., 2001). These tests generally are administered individually to children using basal and ceiling rules that allow items to be tailored to children's current grade level, age, and/or estimated ability level. These comprehensive achievement tests have a number of benefits and limitations. They are beneficial as they provide detailed information regarding children's skills across multiple domains and at different levels of achievement; however, they are costly and time consuming to administer. Thus, it is not realistic for schools to measure achievement across all students in this way.

Nonetheless, as academic achievement and learning are a top priority for schools, the measurement of achievement benchmarks is crucial (also refer to the Accountability section in this chapter). As a result, a popular and widespread method of measuring children's achievement is through standardized testing (rather than individual comprehensive achievement tests, which then are reserved for instances where children are exhibiting signs of exceptionalities). Generally, such standardized testing are a consequence of schools being held accountable for children's academic achievement, rather being used to monitor individual students' performance and adjusting their curricula accordingly. Standardized testing can provide consistent standards across schools (which can be a benefit for children who must change schools frequently). Further, such testing can play a direct role in whether children will attend mandatory summer school courses and/or be allowed to move on to the next grade. Such testing also can play an indirect role in a variety of other areas, including funding for schools, teacher evaluations, and surrounding community real estate markets. Although academic achievement is rightfully a crucial aspect of the education process, Merrow (2001) questions whether high standardized test scores and a high school ranking within a community is enough to determine how children are doing and brings attention to other important issues, such as student engagement and children's emotional and intellectual safety. Given the complexity of children's typical (and atypical) development, these issues are important as well.

## Other Development Issues Relevant to Schools

Although most would consider academic achievement to be the primary role that schools have in children's lives, others suggest that children's social and emotional development also should be targeted so that children can be successful in their school settings (Eastin, 2008). In addition to striving to produce students who are highly literate, intellectually stimulated, and committed to life-long learning, high quality education also should focus on building social skills; promoting positive, safe, and healthy behaviors; and helping children learn to regulate their emotions (Greenberg et al., 2003). Each of these goals can be considered components of social-emotional competence.

In particular, social-emotional competence can be defined as a combination of cooperative and prosocial behaviors, the initiation and maintenance of peer friendships and adult relationships, the management of conflict and aggression, the development of a sense of self-worth, and the mastery of emotional regulation (Aviles, Anderson, and Davila, 2006). In fact, young children depend on their relationships with adults (e.g., parents, caregivers, teachers) to learn about themselves and the world in which they live. Further, child-caregiver relationships have a greater impact on young children's learning than educational toys or preschool curricula (Thompson and Happold, 2002). Most importantly, children's early relationships with their caregivers set the stage for their later social-emotional development and for their cognitive development and academic achievement as well (Whitted, 2011). Thus, it is essential that the promotion of social-emotional development in the school setting begins as early as possible.

*The Preschool Years as a Starting Point for Social-Emotional Instruction.* Settings that support children's social-emotional development are nurturing environments that set children up for future academic success (Aviles et al., 2006). In order to be prepared optimally for increasing academic demands, children must feel curiosity and excitement toward the learning process and must receive positive feedback to build their confidence (Boyd et al., 2005). For many young children in the United States, a large portion of their time is spent in the Preschool setting. Thus, Preschool environments should promote the development of the social-emotional skills that will be needed in later school settings and throughout the lifespan. In particular, caregivers who are warm and responsive are more likely to promote these skills (Boyd et al., 2005). Through relationships with these early caregivers, children gain an understanding of their behaviors and emotions. Children also rely on these relationships to help them identify and interpret what they are feeling (Aviles et al., 2006).

Especially during early childhood, self-regulation is an important component of social-emotional development. Self-regulation involves children learning to manage their own behavior, such that they can withstand impulses, maintain focus, and complete tasks despite the presence of more attractive alternatives (Boyd et al., 2005). In fact, self-regulation underlies almost every task that children face in the Preschool setting, from engaging with peers to paying attention and staying on task. Further, development of self-regulation becomes increasingly important as children grow and transition to Kindergarten and later grades. For example, research shows that levels of self-regulation predict school success in First Grade, over and above children's cognitive skills and their family backgrounds (Raver and Knitzer, 2002). Cognitive self-regulation also is linked to children's achievement throughout school (Boyd et al., 2005). Further, children who are lacking emotional self-regulation are at higher risk for disciplinary problems and are less likely to experience a smooth transition from Preschool to Kindergarten (Boyd et al., 2005). Given these findings, children's development of self-regulation appears to be quite important for their later academic achievement.

The Preschool years also are a sensitive period for learning how to regulate feelings of aggression. Children who exhibit high levels of aggression during their early years are at higher risk for engaging in violent behavior during adolescence (Raver, 2002). Children who display difficult, disruptive behavior (i.e., poor social-emotional skills) are at risk for many potential reasons. For example, teachers may find it more difficult to teach these children, resulting in teachers providing less feedback. Peers also may reject these children, cutting off an important avenue of proper social-emotional development. Finally, these children may lose interest in school and in learning when they are faced with rejection from teachers and peers, resulting in reduced attendance and poor outcomes (Raver, 2002). Overall, social-emotional development begins extremely early in children's lives and needs to be fostered in nurturing environments throughout their school years so that they can achieve academic success.

*Addressing Social-Emotional Development in School.* Research suggests that problems with social-emotional functioning often occur concurrently with academic problems (Barbarin, 2002). For example, social-emotional competence is related directly to school readiness, and school readiness is paramount in the transition to Kindergarten, early school success, and even later achievement in the workplace (NIMH, 2000). Thus, academic development cannot be separated from social-emotional development. In fact, these two domains of development are dynamic and interrelated areas that are necessary for children to be successful in multiple contexts, especially in school (Aviles et al., 2006). Nonetheless, an increasing percentage of Kindergarten teachers reports that their students do not have the social-emotional or behavioral skills to succeed (Boyd et al., 2005). In a national study of over 3,000 Kindergarten teachers, 20 percent of teachers report that at least half of their students have difficulties with social skills (Rimm-Kaufman, Pianta, and Cox, 2000). Unfortunately, these findings have implications for the outcomes experienced by children, as children who do not learn the skills needed for social-emotional competence are at higher risk for falling behind at school and facing academic, social-emotional, and behavioral problems (Aviles et al., 2006).

Even with the relationship between social-emotional competence and academic achievement, most schools are not fostering social-emotional development or strong connections with peers and nurturing adults (DeAngelis, 2010). Less than a third of students in the Sixth through Twelfth Grades report that their schools provide caring, encouraging environments. In addition, just under a third of High School students report engaging in high-risk behaviors (e.g., substance abuse, sex, violence, suicide attempts; Dryfoos, 1997), suggesting the need for greater attention to social-emotional development. According to the National Center for Education Statistics (2002), social-emotional factors also are contributing significantly to high school drop-out rates (35.0%), not getting along with teachers and peers (20.1%), feeling left out (23.2%), and not feeling safe (12.1%). Thus, the need to focus on social-emotional development in school settings is becoming increasingly clear.

*Social-Emotional Learning (SEL) Programs.* Social-emotional learning (SEL) is an approach that has been developed to create a more enriching school environment for our children. In particular, these programs suggest that schools should be invested in teaching students to work with others, to regulate their emotions, to solve problems constructively, and to become better equipped to deal with life's difficulties (DeAngelis, 2010). Proponents of SEL believe that, if schools can teach children and adolescents to work well with others, regulate their emotions, and solve problems constructively, they will be better equipped to handle the challenges that occur in their lives. These goals are best accomplished through effective classroom instruction; student engagement in positive activities in and out of the classroom; and student, parent, and community involvement in program planning, implementation, and evaluation (Greenberg et al., 2003). Ideally, SEL instruction should start in the Preschool years and continue through High School graduation.

Numerous SEL programs have been implemented throughout the United States, each focusing on developing core competencies, including self-awareness, social awareness, self management, relationship skills, and responsible decision making (DeAngelis, 2010). Instead of focusing on a single negative behavior (e.g., drug use, sexual risk taking), these programs take a broad approach and work to understand the common source of such issues (i.e., the lack of social-emotional competencies). SEL often is referred to as the 'missing piece' of education, as it represents the part of education that links academic knowledge with a set of skills necessary for many domains of life (Elias, 2006). Research shows that students are the most responsive academically to classrooms and schools that are non-threatening, that challenge them without discouraging them, and that allow them to feel cared for and valued (Elias, 2006; Osterman, 2000; Zins and Elias, 2006). So that such environments can be fostered, students, parents, educators, and community members should act as partners in planning, implementing, and evaluating SEL initiatives.

In fact, there is a solid and increasing amount of evidence that well-designed, well-implemented SEL initiatives can influence positively children's educational experience. Such programs also appear to improve students' mental health and behavior, to improve students' social competence, and to make the school climate more positive (DeAngelis, 2010). Key strategies that optimize social-emotional development in the classroom include teaching children to apply SEL skills and ethical principles in daily life through interactive classroom instruction; providing frequent opportunities for student self-direction, participation, and school or community service; fostering respectful, successful relationships with peers, teachers, and parents; and supporting and rewarding healthy social-emotional and academic behaviors through systematic school-family-community partnerships (Greenberg et al., 2003). A special synergy is created when SEL programs are implemented, as children learn to foster their own well-being and subsequently become more resilient. These outcomes result in a more positive classroom climate that engages children actively in the learning process (DeAngelis, 2010). When children are more absorbed in what they are learning in their classrooms, they tend to do better in school.

Although SEL programs are gaining popularity and empirical support, they are far from perfect. The Collaborative for Academic, Social, and Emotional Learning (CASEL), a nonprofit organization founded in 1994 and dedicated to improving the science and evidence-base of SEL programs across the country, places only 22 of the United States' several hundred SEL programs on its exemplary list of being well-designed and evidence-based (DeAngelis, 2010). Further, schools have to be willing to include SEL programs in their curricula and foster their success. Research is being conducted currently to understand how to best implement SEL programs and to identify which factors reinforce the adoption of, adherence to, and sustainability of such interventions (Zins and Elias, 2006). The implementation of such programs may seem prohibitive, however, given some of the challenges (e.g., funding issues) that schools are facing currently. Nonetheless, other challenges (e.g., managing children's behavior problems) could be best served with SEL programs.

## Challenges

Clearly, schools should play important roles in developing children's academic achievement as well as their social-emotional skills. Nonetheless, schools are facing currently several challenges that make it difficult to fulfill their obligations to our children. Some of these challenges will be presented here in an effort to present a picture of how difficult it is for schools to serve the needs of our children today. The challenges presented here are not meant to be an exhaustive list. Instead, the challenges presented here appear to the authors to be some of the most important challenges that have the capacity to affect children adversely.

## Funding

With current budget concerns, schools clearly are being asked to do more for our children with less funding. Since 2008, budget cuts in elementary and secondary education have impacted greatly 34 states and the District of Columbia (Johnson, Oliff, and Williams, 2011). Due to the current economic recession, schools in the United States are facing funding crises as tax revenue decreases and federal stimulus money expires. For example, in 2008, Central Florida public schools faced significant funding cuts, with counties facing significant losses (e.g., Orange County, Florida, faced a $70 million dollar loss from the state; Hobbs, 2008). In other words, local school districts in Florida experienced a funding cut of $140 per student in 2008 (Johnson, Oliff, and Koulish, 2008). In addition, in 2011, Colorado public schools faced an even higher budget cut of $400 per student, equating to a 5 percent decrease in funding from 2010 and a total decrease of $260 million (Johnson et al., 2011). Core classroom programs throughout the country that were funded previously by federal stimulus dollars also may lose nearly $1.2 billion in 2012 (Deslatte and Garcia, 2011). As a result of these losses, schools have lost positions, are forfeiting enrichment classes (e.g., Physical Education, Art), are going without supplies, and sometimes are finding it necessary to close (Hobbs, 2008).

Teachers especially are feeling the effects of education budget cuts. In the current economic climate, many believe that spending must decrease so that the national deficit can decrease. As a result, the funding for countless programs around the country is being cut. Recently, many states are reducing spending by exempting local school districts from class size requirements, thus increasing teachers' workloads and stress (Johnson et al., 2011). To reduce spending further, during the 2009-2010 school year, teachers in Hawaii were forced to teach more material in a shorter period of time because the state shortened the school year by 17 days and then furloughed teachers for this time (Johnson et al., 2011). Teaching positions also are being sacrificed due to budget cuts and funding limitations. The National Education Association (2011) reports that grants to local educational agencies may soon be cut by $693.5 million, potentially eliminating over 9,100 education jobs in the very near future. For example, Texas is aiming to reduce spending in 2011 by making up to 100,000 layoffs in the state's school system (Krugman, 2011). In addition, early intervention and special education programs are being cut, and professional development programs (particularly professional development in science instruction) for teachers and principals also are being eliminated from many states' school systems (Griffith and Scharmann, 2008; Johnson et al.,

2011). Further, in 2011, teachers in Seminole County, Florida, will receive a one-time bonus (ranging from $600-$1,900) in place of a salary pay-raise (Weber, 2011). Thus, funding issues have an effect on schools as well as the professionals who work there.

Funding cuts in the areas of health, physical education, and nutrition in schools also are impacting our children greatly. Many studies show that children's academic performance is related significantly to their physical fitness and nutrition (Florence, Asbridge, and Veugelers, 2008; Shilts, Lamp, Horowitz, and Townsend, 2009; Whittberg, Northrup, and Cottrel, 2009). For example, Florence and colleagues (2008) indicate that increased student nutrition and diet quality are related to a decreased likelihood of literacy test failure. Schools initially were able to make some accommodations to capitalize on this relationship. For example, over 31 million children received their lunches each day from the National School Lunch Program in 2009, to the benefit of these children. Nonetheless, although school breakfast programs increase children's school attendance and decrease tardiness, it is often a struggle to properly fund local and national health and nutrition initiatives for school-age children (Taras, 2005; U.S. Department of Agriculture, 2010). For example, the National School Lunch Program (NSLP) provides cash subsidies to schools for every meal that the school serves as long as the schools offer free or reduced price lunches to eligible students (U.S. Department of Agriculture, 2010). Although the School Food Authority's (SFA) revenue covered the reported costs of the school lunch program, only 82 percent of the program's full cost was covered by the SFA's revenue (U.S. Department of Agriculture, 2008).

Physical education also is of great importance to student health but currently is facing budget cuts in schools across the country. Many studies show that increased physical fitness (i.e., aerobic activity and muscular fitness) is related to increased academic success (Eveland-Sayers, Farley, Fuller, Morgan, and Caputo, 2009; Wittberg, Cottrell, Davis, and Northrup, 2010; Wittberg, Northrup, and Cottrel, 2008). Because schools' funding often depends on standardized test performance, physical education and recess time often are subject to elimination due to cost and/or time constraints. Wittberg and colleagues (2009) indicate that deemphasizing physical education in schools and increasing emphasis on curriculum-based education in order to improve standardized test scores may be ineffective and perhaps detrimental. Additionally, enrichment classes (i.e. art and music education) are experiencing funding cuts for similar reasons. Schools are highly unlikely to spend what little funding they have on subjects where their students will not be tested. High performance in art and music will not garner adequate or competitive funding at public schools in the United States; thus, schools have little funding to dedicate to these enrichment programs (Beveridge, 2010). In turn, these programs unfortunately face discontinuation.

Similarly, when states adjusted to meet the new standards required by No Child Left Behind (NCLB), a strong emphasis was placed on math and reading education, thus decreasing emphasis on science and writing education (Eastin, 2008; Griffith and Scharmann, 2008). Consequently, funding for science and writing education has declined markedly across the country as schools attempt to reach the standards set by NCLB. For example, because schools' funding often depends largely upon the improvement of math and reading test scores, teachers report that both current funding and time is dedicated more often to those subjects that are linked to future funding. As a result, funding is inadequate for the instruction of science as well as the creativity that it requires (Griffith and Scharmann, 2008; Harmon, 2011). Eastin (2008) also reports that, because students' skills in writing, science, and social science are tested in only two grades between Kindergarten and Eighth Grade, these subjects tend to be emphasized more strongly when they will be evaluated. Such procedures are followed especially in lower-performing schools, where funding is scarce for subjects that are not being tested in every grade (Eastin, 2008). By teaching such subjects only when they will be evaluated, the need for funding in these subject areas is decreased, resulting in decreased spending. It is apparent, however, that these kinds of procedures are detrimental to the futures of our children. Although it makes fiscal sense to cut non-tested subjects first, this lack of information will harm our children in the long term. These tendencies also suggest that school curricula are being driven less by the needs of our children and more by accountability.

## Accountability

Beyond issues with funding affecting the education of our children, legislation also has moved to make teachers more accountable for the information that is being taught in their classrooms and for what our children are actually learning. As a result, accountability also may be considered a current challenge for schools in the United States, although some may disagree with this statement.

*Historical Background of Accountability in Schools.* Accountability has a basis in educational reform across the past several decades. The origins of government educational reform began with the Elementary and Secondary Education Act of 1965 (ESEA). As a part of Lyndon B. Johnson's War on Poverty and Great Society programs, ESEA was historically groundbreaking in that it shifted certain educational decisions, which primarily had been regulated by state and local parties, to federal entities, who then were in charge of the allocation of funding and the spearheading of public school policy decisions (Duffy, Giordano, Farrell, Paneque, and Crump, 2008). This act followed the Supreme Court decision of *Brown Versus the Board of Education*. This case was involved in the desegregation of schools and was based on the idea that access to quality education alone was not sufficient for students to learn appropriately. As a result, ESEA allocated money to communities with the greatest need, as it was believed that the achievement gap between students who were from higher socioeconomic backgrounds and those who were from lower socioeconomic backgrounds could be closed with the right support and interventions (e.g., Title I; Meier and Wood, 2004). One billion dollars were distributed in 1965 to schools and districts, primarily based on child poverty data (Duffy et al., 2008). However, allocating federal funds in this way failed to be the panacea for addressing the achievement gap between students who were from higher socioeconomic backgrounds and those who were from lower socioeconomic backgrounds. In addition, misappropriation of funds resulting from ambiguity in the law and a lack of oversight led Congress to amend the law four times between 1965 and 1980 (Thomas and Brady, 2005).

During the Ronald Reagan administration in the 1980's, federal funding and the role of the federal government in public education was reduced greatly (Duffy et al., 2008). During this period, states took the lead in reforming public school policies, shifting to tougher academic standards, additional course requirements, longer school days, and changes in the preparation of teachers (National Commission on Excellence in Education, 1983). In 1988, Title I of ESEA (i.e., funding distribution to schools with disadvantaged students) was amended. These changes required states to document the academic achievement of disadvantaged students through standardized testing, with funds allocated based on disadvantaged students' reported academic achievement (Duffy et al., 2008). The push for accountability in schools continued with George Bush's America 2000 Excellence Education Act of 1991. This piece of legislation was designed to establish greater accountability based on higher academic standards and more flexibility in the allocation of federal funds (Thomas and Brady, 2005). Although this legislation was not passed by Congress, it fueled the reform initiatives that were underway in some states.

Later legislation incorporated a role for accountability as well. The Goals 2000: Education America Act (1994) emphasized a standards-based education system where the standards and expectations were the same for all students. This act also used academic achievement levels as an indicator for the success of reform efforts (Duffy et al., 2008). States were required to establish academic standards for each grade level and to create standardized tests that could measure whether students were meeting those standards in elementary, middle, and high school grades (Hess and Petrilli, 2006). In addition, school districts were required for the first time to report their schools that did not make adequate yearly progress (AYP). School districts also were required to formally improve schools that were not making AYP (Duffy et al., 2008).

In 2000, Congress determined that the billions of dollars that had been allocated to ESEA had not had a significant effect on narrowing the achievement gap between student who were from higher socioeconomic backgrounds and those who were from lower socioeconomic backgrounds (Thomas and Brady, 2005). The result of this decision was a push for even greater accountability in public schools. In conjunction with these events, No Child Left Behind (NCLB; 2002), which was developed and enacted by the George W. Bush administration, reauthorized and renamed ESEA. NCLB continued to include provisions for greater accountability for students' performance and for empowering parents with choice options. This act also included newly emphasized research-based practices, a reduction in bureaucracy, and increased flexibility in spending. Further, NCLB redefined the federal government's role in education, as it granted the federal government the authority to determine the appropriateness of state standards and accountability systems, to establish a national timeline for all schools to meet achievement goals, and to offer solutions to schools and students who did not meet the goals within the specified time frame (Hess and Petrilli, 2006).

*Race to the Top.* More recently, educational legislation and accountability have been revisited again. As part of the American Recovery and Reinvestment Act of 2009 (i.e., the 'stimulus bill'), the Barack Obama administration provided $4.35 billion to the Department of Education for the 'Race to the Top' (RTT) program. This program, which is based on a model of competition, allowed states to apply for funds from the Department of Education to implement educational reform. Forty states and the District of Columbia entered the competition, and 16 states were finalists. Two states, Delaware and Tennessee, then were winners of the first round of the competition. Delaware and Tennessee won $100 million and $500 million, respectively, for being awarded the most points out of the 500 hundred points available. Points were awarded for compliance with policies consistent with those of the Department of Education (e.g., using data to improve instruction) in a number of categories (e.g., great teachers and leaders) and subcategories (e.g., developing and implementing common, high quality assessments; U. S. Department of Education, 2011).

This competition for education funding was proposed as an objective and scientific review process that would be based on the precise numerical scores provided by five review panelists. Following the first round of funding distribution for RTT, some argued that the review process for awarding states points for funding is arbitrary and subjective as well as subject more to bias and chance than superior compliance with reform policies (Peterson and Rothstein, 2010). One current problem with the RTT review process is that, in order to receive more points and a better likelihood of funding from RTT, some states (e.g., Pennsylvania) would have to downplay support and funding for research supported programs (e.g., early childhood school preparation) that it implements currently. Instead, they would have to focus on categories in the RTT scoring system that receive more points but have weaker research support. Additionally, some argue that the RTT method of distribution for educational funding is misguided, as the substitution of competition for uniform funding may be detrimental for states in current economic crisis (Peterson and Rothstein, 2010). In order to compete for funding, states must allocate significant time and resources to the application process itself, further stretching the limited educational funding available to states suffering from economic crisis. Further, the review process for funding may be exploited by states that make small changes in their application in order to take advantage of specific quirks in the rating system rather than making changes that reflect actual improvement in state educational policies (Peterson and Rothstein, 2010).

The Obama administration proposed that this type of competition for funding should be the new model for federal education spending. Further, this administration proposed a freezing of the formula-driven Title I funding at its present level without future adjustment for inflation and suggested that increases in federal education funding should be exclusive to a new collection of competitive grants, similar to RTT requirements. With the current economic recession and its impact on education quality, however, reductions in real Title I funding could further exacerbate state fiscal crises (Peterson and Rothstein, 2010). In addition, the initial RTT competitive funding system has proven to have little credibility in its funding distribution methods (Peterson and Rothstein, 2010). Therefore, some argue that a pass-fail system, rather than a points system, to determine which states should receive federal funding awards for compliance with federal educational policies and for undertaking reasonable efforts to improve their educational system should be implemented (Peterson and Rothstein, 2010). Although this type of system will not eliminate completely the errors in the current system, such a system would allow more states who are making the effort to 'race to the top' to receive funding.

*Standardizing Education and the Overemphasis on 'One-Size-Fits All' Teaching and Learning.* A critical, but hidden, assumption of the NCLB system of accountability is that increasing demands and expectations for students will result in, or cause, increased student and teacher performance. Many have argued, however, that this notion is too simplistic when applied to the complexity of human learning, especially in a nation as diverse as the United States (Duffy et al., 2008). In addition, NCLB mandates that only programs that have been proven scientifically to produce positive effects are eligible for funding. Essentially, NCLB suggests that we can specify what all children at each grade level should know and learn in their academic subjects. In actuality, however, what children should learn in school can be subjective. Further, when children do not reach this predetermined standard of what they should know, whether it be due to longitudinal effects of sociocultural factors, poor schools, or intellectual or learning disabilities, the consequences involve lost funding to the very schools that need it the most to improve our children's learning (Duffy et al., 2008).

One effect of NCLB and its push for greater accountability through high-stakes standardized testing is the way in which schools and teachers must adapt their methods of distributing knowledge, as there is always a need to meet the AYP standards. When the yardstick for student academic achievement becomes based on one particular set of knowledge (e.g., in Florida, FCAT tests for reading and mathematics), teachers become even more likely to assess and work with their students in an acontextual way, minimizing the focus on the context and culture of individual students (Duffy et al., 2008). In particular, high-stakes standardized testing limits the curricula and the creativity of teachers in the delivery of their curricula and limits the ability of teachers to differentiate their teaching. As a result, it becomes more difficult to accommodate for a diverse group of students in terms of their cultural, linguistic, social-emotional, physical, and experiential differences (Duffy et al., 2008).

Many emphasize that teaching acontextually and consequently devaluing differentiated teaching methods is especially problematic for children in a nation as diverse as the United States (Duffy et al., 2008). Some argue that the emphasis on acontextual and quantitatively-oriented methods of teaching and assessment seem to contradict the main purpose of NCLB (i.e., the narrowing of the achievement gap among diverse groups), as it minimizes the importance of differentiated and culturally-relevant teaching methods and assessment (Shaw, 2005). In addition, the concept of mandated assessments further implies that certain kinds of experiences and knowledge are valued over others, resulting in a 'one-size-fits-all' approach to knowledge and learning (Duffy et al., 2008). Further, the emphasis on mastering basic skills (limited in this situation to reading and math) reduces the likelihood of our children's exposure to other experiences (e.g., music, art, physical education, recess) through time and funding constraints. These restrictions become obvious as teachers and districts feel the pressure to eliminate time and resources for curricula that are not assessed on mandated high-stakes standardized testing (Sunderman, Kim, and Orfield, 2005).

*Accountability and Diverse Students.* Well before the implementation of high-stakes standardized testing on a national level with NCLB, standardized tests have shown consistent differences in outcome for varying socioeconomic, racial, and ethnic groups (as noted earlier in this chapter). With the exception of Asian Americans, ethnic minority populations continue to score significantly lower on traditional standardized tests relative to Caucasian Americans (Onwuegbuzie and Daly, 2001; Roth, Bevier, Bobko, Switzer, and Tyler, 2001). For example, the Scholastic Aptitude Test (SAT), a standardized test widely used by colleges and universities to make admissions decisions, continues to demonstrate a 12 to 15 percent gap between Caucasian students and their racial and ethnic counterparts. This gap is evident even when the socioeconomic status of the students is controlled (Gandara and Lopez, 1998; Holman, 1995). Further, the observations of teachers who use culturally responsive teaching strategies suggest that the outcomes of standardized assessments frequently contradict what teachers observe and assess in the classroom (Hood, 1998). Although research suggests that culturally-sensitive and differentiated teaching and assessment can mitigate the achievement gap found through standardized testing, this type of teaching and assessment is difficult to implement in public school systems, particularly in conjunction with the NCLB system of accountability (Newman and Associates, 1996).

Language proficiency also provides a setback for some children in demonstrating their knowledge and achievement gains in high-stakes standardized testing. Studies suggest that children who gain proficiency in the 'language' of the test and with the testing environment fare better. Further, actively attempting to improve children's proficiency with the language of the test improves their outcomes (Buriel, Perez, DeMent, Chavez, and Moran, 1998). Therefore, one of the difficulties related to the validity of standardized testing outcomes is that children who are lacking in proficiency with Caucasian, middle-class English ultimately will be at a disadvantage from the start (Altshuler and Schmautz, 2006). Congress recognized the impact of language on children's assessment performance and required the recent reauthorization of the Individuals with Disabilities Education Act (IDEA 2004). IDEA states that all assessments should be developed in children's native language. Nonetheless, this requirement does not circumvent the difficulties experienced by children who have specific, and often unrecognized, English dialects within the American culture (Altshuler and Kopels, 2003). For example, learning and assessment difficulties related to dialect are documented for students who speak Appalachian or certain African American dialects at home and who must learn Caucasian, middle-class English in school to succeed (Gopaul-McNicol, Reid, and Wisdom, 1998; Siegel, 1999).

In addition, the effects of school accountability may be problematic for another group of diverse children, those with intellectual and learning disabilities. IDEA requires an appropriate public education in the least restrictive environment for children who have disabilities. Although IDEA focuses on the individualization of learning, the most recent reauthorization of this act emphasizes access for children who have disabilities to general education curricula and to participation in general large scale assessments in line with NCLB (Bouck, 2009). Although research suggests that better post-schooling outcomes occur when a functional curriculum (e.g., daily living skills, functional academics, independent living skills) is provided to students who have intellectual disabilities, functional curricula goals do not align well with the accountability goals and assessment requirements of NCLB (Bouck, 2009). Therefore, the application of a functional curriculum for children who have intellectual disabilities appears to be a disadvantage for school districts as well as for the children themselves, as it would be unfair to test children on content knowledge that they have not been taught. These factors have caused some to wonder whether the policies of NCLB, with its emphasis on accountability and general education curricula, have lost sight of the original basis for public education, which is to develop productive and responsible citizens for a democratic society (Brick, 2005; Cuban, 2003).

*Research on the Effects of Accountability for Improving Education Standards.* Data shows that some progress was made in the 1970's and 1980's with regard to narrowing achievement gaps across ethnic groups (i.e., the math achievement gap between African American and Caucasian individuals was reduced by half; Lee, 2006). There was a major setback in this progress, however, in the 1990's, leading to the reform of ESEA through NCLB. In order to understand whether the external accountability policies of NCLB have their intended impact, it is necessary to compare how well the nation and states accomplished academic excellence and equity before and after NCLB. Analysis of these trends demonstrates that NCLB did not have a significant impact on improving reading and math achievement. In particular, national averages for mathematics test scores remain similar to pre-NCLB levels, and reading scores have stagnated (Lee, 2006). These facts, as well as the fact that many states had implemented their own school accountability systems prior to NCLB, prompt some to conclude erroneously that NCLB goals are being accomplished. In fact, data reveal that states using test-driven external accountability either before or after NCLB do not have reductions in racial or income inequalities for achievement in reading or math and that the achievement gap between these groups continues unchanged (Lee, 2006).

Further, compared to the National Assessment of Educational Progress (NAEP), state assessments tend to inflate their overall proficiency level and deflate their achievement gap among racial groups. These results imply that states utilizing high-stakes standardized testing policies prior to NCLB adopt relatively lower performance standards. Such standards result in an over-estimation of proficiency rates and an underestimation of the achievement gap. Thus, data on the effects of the implementation of high-stakes account-ability indicate that these standards have not had the impact on the very groups who they were put in place to help.

Further, high-stakes assessment appears to lead schools to make decisions that impact their scores. Certainly, this consequence was not foreseen when NCLB was implemented. For instance, equity promoting through the 'grading' of schools has led to schools making certain decisions to maintain their status and, therefore, their funding. Such decisions may include placing struggling students on lower tracks or encouraging them to drop out so that they do not impact negatively their schools' grades (Duffy et al., 2008). Additionally, children and teachers from schools with low or failing grades can be stigmatized by their schools' grades. Parents often do not get the choice to move their children from schools that are failing to schools that are succeeding if the succeeding schools do not wish to grant access to these children from failing schools. Certainly, the concern may be that these children may lower their successful grade. Children also may be retained in their grade if their scores are below average so that they do not negatively affect the average score of the next grade. Ironically, these children are often in the groups that the original legislation was targeting to assist.

## Educating Boys versus Girls

Beyond considering funding and accountability, challenges in education also must consider the characteristics of those children who are attending schools. One such characteristic that has important implications for education today is children's gender. Given the need for higher education today, academic achievement is imperative for both boys and girls (Eastin, 2008). Historically, boys surpassed girls in many areas of academic achievement based on a variety of factors, including limited educational opportunities, societal perceptions of the roles that girls played in society, teachers' perceptions of girls' academic achievement, and poor self-concept with regard to girls' own academic achievement abilities (Eisenhart and Finkel, 1998; Sadker and Sadker, 1994). Research now suggests, however, that the academic achievement gap between boys and girls has turned in favor of girls (Silverman, 2003). In fact, research focusing on education from Kindergarten through Twelfth Grade indicates that girls are attaining higher grades, achieving higher levels of education (e.g., Duckworth and Seligman, 2006; Silverman, 2003), and are more likely to be involved in academically oriented groups relative to boys (Sommers, 2000).

Research also is showing that boys are failing to remain engaged in their educational activities when compared to girls. For example, boys are trailing behind girls academically and are less likely to attend college (Chamberlin, 2008). In addition, the National Center for Education Statistics (2002) reports that nearly twice as many boys relative to girls who are between the ages of 5- and 12-years are held back from progressing to the next grade (Freeman, 2004). Further, by the age of 17-years, boys are nearly twice as likely to be suspended from school when compared to girls (Office of Juvenile Justice and Delinquency Prevention, 2006). As such, the abovementioned research indicates that boys may currently be at a disadvantage within their respective school settings.

Accordingly, research is examining the factors that may be associated with boys falling behind in their current school settings (e.g., Duckworth and

Seligman, 2006; Silverman, 2003; Sommers, 2000). Some research suggests that girls may be performing better than they did in the past. Such improvements may contribute to the appearance that boys are falling behind (see Mead, 2006, for a review). Research indicates that girls' higher performance in their current school settings may be a result of changes in societal expectations for girls (i.e., girls should continue on to higher education) as well as changes in teachers' expectations for girls' academic achievement (e.g., Weaver-Hightower, 2003). A large body of research, however, shows that girls are performing better in their current school settings than they have historically *and* that boys are failing to engage in their current educational opportunities relative to their performance in school historically (Chamberlin, 2008). As such, some research suggests that the overall changes that are being made to school curricula may be influencing boys' performance in their current school settings negatively but may not having the same detrimental effect on girls' performance in school (e.g., Duckworth and Seligman, 2006; Silverman, 2003; Sommers, 2000).

With regard to changes in current school settings, there appears to be a trend toward increased overall structure and high levels of scheduling for children in school and after school in an effort to increase children's academic performance (Elkind, 2001; Hirsh-Pasek and Golinkoff, 2003). In addition, schools in the United States are reducing the amount of free play available during the school day (Pellegrini, 2002; Pellegrini and Bohn, 2005) in order to increase the time allotted to focus on children's performance in academic subjects, such as reading and math (Dillon, 2006; Elias and Arnold, 2006). Research suggests, however, that boys' development, particularly in the domain of motor abilities and social interaction skills, benefits from active play, something that is increasingly being discouraged in schools today (Chamberlin, 2008). Thus, the reduction in active play at school may actually hinder children's academic performance, particularly that of boys. Given that research suggests that unstructured play at school can help to promote children's cognitive and social-emotional development, particularly for boys, it is concerning that children's opportunities for play are being restricted (Gross-Loh, 2007).

This trend of increasing overall structure for children may be particularly problematic for boys for several reasons. Research indicates that children's ability to pay attention and regulate their behavior is important for classroom functioning (Blair, 2002) and academic success (Howse, Calkins, Anastopoulos, Keane, and Shelton, 2003). For example, higher scores on reading and math assessments are related to children's regulation of their behavior and their greater attentional skills (Blair and Razza, 2007). Given that boys are already consistently rated by parents and teachers as having higher observed activity levels and problems with inattention relative to girls (Rescorla, Achenbach, Ginzburg, et al., 2007; Rescorla, Achenbach, Ivanova, et al., 2007), the move toward an increase in structure and less active play time may decrease behavioral regulation and attentional abilities for boys who may already be struggling in these areas. For example, in a study examining teachers' reports of behaviors problems, boys scored higher in eight separate areas (e.g., Attention Deficit/Hyperactivity Problems, Oppositional Defiant Problems, Conduct Problems; Rescorla, Achenbach, Ginzburg, et al., 2007). Given that boys are rated as having a more difficult time with the regulation of externalizing behaviors as well as with inattention, assessment scores may be influenced negatively by the increased structure of the school curriculum.

Given that the structure of the school day is changing, with decreases in physical activity (e.g., Elkind, 2001; Hirsh-Pasek and Golinkoff, 2003; Pellegrini, 2002; Pellegrini and Bohn, 2005), teachers may be more likely to observe behaviors such as hyperactivity and increased inattention. These behaviors may be attributed to the increase in structure and the lack of free time during the school day, rather than a dramatic increase in certain behaviors over the past several decades. Consequently, teachers may be more likely to overidentify children as having behavior problems in today's school settings (Glass and Wegar, 2000; Havey, Olson, McCormick, and Cates, 2005). Given that boys are already more likely to be rated as having externalizing problems (Rescorla, Achenbach, Ginzburg, et al., 2007; Rescorla, Achenbach, Ivanova, et al., 2007), they may be at increased risk for being improperly targeted as having behavior problems in current school settings (e.g., Glass and Wegar, 2000; Havey et al., 2005) due to the changes being made in school curricula.

In turn, these changes may have consequences for boys' academic achievement, for their peer acceptance, and for their own self-concept of their academic abilities (for a review, see Campbell, 1995). For example, children who are targeted as having social-emotional or behavior problems are more likely to be alienated from their peers (Coolahan, Fantuzzo, Mendez, and McDermott, 2008) and to be perceived negatively by their teachers (Wentzel and Asher, 1995). Thus, the overidentification of emotional and behavioral problems can lead to negative perceptions by teachers and peers (e.g., Campbell, 1995; Coolahan et al., 2008; Wentzel and Asher, 1995). Such negative perceptions from others can influence children's own perceptions of their ability to succeed in school (e.g., Campbell, 1995) and ultimately contribute to a decrease in motivation for academic success (e.g., Steinberg,

1996). Accordingly, it is vital that school curricula focus on academic subjects as well as recognize the interplay between academic success and the structure of the school day in relation to optimal conditions for academic success for both boys and girls. In addition, it is vitally important that behavior problems exhibited by children in school settings are identified accurately and managed properly, as all children deserve an opportunity to learn to the best of their ability.

## Identifying and Managing Behaviors in the Classroom

Teachers often are primary sources of information regarding reports of children's emotional and behavioral functioning (e.g., when diagnosing Attention-Deficit/Hyperactivity Disorder [ADHD]; Havey et al., 2005). In particular, observing children's behavior in their current school settings (e.g., in the classroom, on the playground) adds greatly to the comprehensive picture of children's functioning in school as well as their need for school-based intervention (Rapport, 2005). It appears, however, that teachers tend to overidentify children as having behavior problems (e.g., ADHD; Glass and Wegar, 2000; Havey et al., 2005). For example, although prevalence estimate for ADHD range from approximately 3 to 5 percent (APA, 2000), Havey and colleagues (2005) find that teachers identify 23.97 percent of children in their classes as meeting criteria for the different subtypes of ADHD (i.e., using the ADHD Rating Scale-IV [School Version]). These ratings have different correlates, with boys being more likely to be identified by teachers and teachers identifying more children from larger classes (Havey et al., 2005).

Other characteristics of teachers also may be relevant to their ratings of children's emotional and behavioral functioning. For example, Liljequist and Renk (2007) suggest that teachers are more likely to be bothered by children's externalizing behavior problems, perhaps making it more likely that teachers would identify these behaviors as being problematic. Further, teachers' sense of their own efficacy in the classroom is related to their ratings of how bothersome children's behavior problems are as well as how much control children are perceived to have over these behavior problems (Liljequist and Renk, 2007). Thus, teachers' feelings about how well they are performing in their school duties may be related closely to their identification of children's emotional and behavioral problems, suggesting that teachers who are doubting their abilities may identify more children as having emotional and behavioral problems.

Given these correlates of teachers' ratings of children's emotional and behavioral problems, mental health consultation may be one way in which teachers can receive assistance with managing children's behavior problems. Such consultation is defined as an ongoing relationship between a mental health professional and a childcare provider or school teacher with the goal of addressing children's difficult behavior and promoting children's healthy social-emotional development (Cohen and Kaufmann, 2000). Further, such consultation may utilize a child- and family-focused model, in which the concerns of a specific child and/or family are addressed. Such consultation also may utilize a program-focused model, in which the overall quality of the classroom environment is increased and strategies are provided to increase school professionals' capacity to address children's emotional and behavioral problems (Cohen and Kaufmann, 2000). Such interventions, particularly in the context of concurrent interventions at home, are effective in treating a variety of children's emotional and behavioral problems (Rork and McNeil, 2008).

In conjunction with seeking assistance in managing children's behavior, teachers tend to rate consultants' skills as being highly effective (MacLeod, Jones, Somers, and Havey, 2001). Generally, school-based consultation also is related to children making gains in academic achievement and social behaviors. Further, MacLeod and colleagues (2001) note that approximately two-thirds of children rated in conjunction with a teacher survey of school-based consultation exhibit improvements in their functioning. In addition, consultants' interpersonal, problem solving, consultation process, and ethical skills tend to be rated as highly effective. Teachers also tend to endorse that consultants having a step-by-step plan, adhering to this treatment plan, and utilizing comparisons of baseline to treatment data are related to children's behavior changes (MacLeod et al., 2001). In addition to being related to improvements in children's behaviors, mental health consultation is related to lower rates of expulsion (Perry, Dunne, McFadden, and Campbell, 2008). In particular, Perry and colleagues (2008) suggest that more than three-quarters of preschoolers who are at risk for expulsion (i.e., mostly as a result of aggressive, disruptive, and inattentive behaviors) but who receive individualized consultation are able to be maintained in their current childcare placement. These children show reduced rates of behavior problems and improvements in their social skills, suggesting that there are improvements in their overall adjustment to their current school environments.

Problems may arise with school-based consultation, however. For example, teachers may be hesitant to allow psychologists into their classrooms and may refuse school-based consultation (Gonzalez, Nelson, Gutkin, and

Shwery, 2004). Consultants' perceptions of teachers' hesitancy suggest that a variety of factors are related to consulting, including teacher factors (e.g., teaching efficacy), psychologist factors (e.g., problem solving skills), the principal's support for the consultation, and the reciprocal nature of the consultation (e.g., teachers being able to serve as a consultant for the psychologist; Gutkin and Hickman, 1990). Thus, psychologists' and teachers' views of each other may play a role in promoting or hindering the effectiveness of school consultation (Rork and McNeil, 2008). Unfortunately, another problem that may arise is that school counselors and psychologists often are cut from budgets (Eastin, 2008). Should such cuts be made, school-based consultation may become relatively unavailable for some school settings.

## Problematic Peer Relationships

Another place in which children's emotional and behavioral problems may manifest themselves is in the context of peer interactions in (and out of) school. The most problematic peer interactions occur in the form of bullying. Bullying can be defined as a form of aggression that is characterized by the intent to harm another, by multiple occurrences of such interactions, and by an imbalance of power between a child who is bullying and a child who is being victimized (Bauman, 2008). Bullying behavior is divided typically into direct and indirect (or relational; e.g., social exclusion, spreading rumors, withholding friendship) bullying. Direct bullying can be further divided into physical bullying, which includes overt acts of aggression (e.g., hitting), and verbal bullying, which includes teasing and verbal threats. Direct bullying traditionally has received more research attention, whereas relational bullying has received less attention until more recently (Bauman and Del Rio, 2006).

In addition to these traditional forms of bullying, a new form of bullying, known as cyberbullying, has emerged with the increased use of electronic forms of communication. Cyberbullying includes the use of e-mails, blogging, and other forms of electronic media to bully others. Given the relatively novel existence of this type of bullying, research on the topic is scarce. Although this form of bullying is just as problematic as more traditional forms of bullying (Hinduja and Patchin, 2010), much of the existing research indicates that it is not as prevalent as other forms of bullying, particularly in current school settings (Bradshaw, Sawyer, and O'Brennan, 2007; Varjas, Henrich, and

Meyers, 2009). Because this type of bullying appears to be more problematic in community settings, it will not be addressed specifically in this section.

Until relatively recently, bullying was considered by many to be a typical childhood event and was not considered to be harmful (Arseneault, Bowest, and Shakoor, 2010). Although interest in bullying has increased, the majority of research has been conducted in countries other than the United States. Recently, the amount of research in the United States on bullying has increased dramatically, however. This increase can be attributed partially to the increased attention that has been given to public school violence (Bauman, 2008). This recent research now shows that bullying is both problematic and widespread. For example, Bradshaw and colleagues (2007) indicate that 49 percent of surveyed students report being bullied during a one month period, with 23 percent reporting two or more instances of bullying. More than half of these students report that bullying is a moderate to serious problem in their schools (Bradshaw et al., 2007). Both direct verbal bullying and relational bullying emerge as the most prevalent forms of problematic peer interactions in recent research (Bradshaw et al., 2007; Carbone-Lopez, Esbensen, and Brick, 2010; Wang, Iannotti, and Nansel, 2009). There appears to be some differences in bullying across boys and girls, however, with boys being much more likely to experience physical victimization and girls being more likely to experience verbal or relational bullying (Carbone-Lopez et al., 2010; Varjas et al., 2009; Wang et al., 2009). According to students' reports, bullying primarily occurs in classrooms, cafeterias, hallways, and bathrooms as well as on playgrounds (Bradshaw et al., 2007; Hughes, Middleton, and Marshall, 2009).

Recent research also indicates that bullying is harmful and that it should be addressed through interventions in school settings (Arseneault et al., 2010). Although longitudinal data on the effects of bullying is very limited, victimization is linked to several negative outcomes, including increased risk for psychopathology, low self-esteem, delinquent behavior, truancy, discipline problems, academic disengagement, and poor grades (Arseneault et al., 2010; Carbone-Lopez et al., 2010; Dukes, Stein, and Zane, 2009; Gastic, 2008; Juvonen, Wang, and Espinoza, 2011). Although both direct and indirect forms of bullying appear to have similar negative outcomes (Dukes et al., 2009), some forms of bullying may be particularly problematic for specific populations. For example, homophobic teasing is related to an increase in depression, suicidal ideation, anxiety, truancy, substance use, and negative school views (Birkett, Espelage, and Koenig, 2009; Swearer, Turner, Givens, and Pollack, 2008). Homophobic teasing also is particularly problematic for boys, who may experience more bullying in the form of homophobic teasing relative to other forms of bullying (Swearer et al., 2008).

Although students report high rates of bullying within their schools, teachers tend to report significantly lower rates of bullying. For example, Bradshaw and colleagues (2007) indicate that, in surveys, teachers report bullying prevalence rates of approximately 15 percent. In addition, teachers are significantly more likely to report bullying than they are to report victimization, which is likely due to the fact that bullying tends to be more salient to teachers (Wienke Totura, Green, Karver, and Gesten, 2009). Although teachers report significantly lower prevalence rates for bullying, it generally still is acknowledged that bullying is a serious problem (Bradshaw et al, 2007). Teachers also are highly likely to intervene when they witness bullying. Their interventions most often take the form of direct coaching or disciplinary action (Bauman, Rigby, and Hoppa, 2008; Bradshaw et al., 2007). The likelihood of teachers intervening, however, may be affected by a number of factors, including school policy and the type of bullying that is witnessed. Specifically, increased teacher preparedness and awareness through clear anti-bullying training and policies appear to lead to a great likelihood of intervention and success in teachers addressing bullying issues (Bauman et al., 2008; Novick and Isaacs, 2010). Nonetheless, with regard to bullying subtypes, teachers may be less likely to recognize relational bullying and to empathize with victims of this type of bullying. It is possible that teachers are less likely to identify relational bullying because these behaviors tend not be governed by clear school policies (Bauman and Del Rio, 2006). Thus, teachers would likely benefit from explicit training in the various types of bullying and from clear expectations regarding how to effectively intervene in a bullying situation.

Although children's own characteristics may be related to whether or not they will be bullied, factors in the school environment drastically increase this likelihood (Arseneault et al., 2010). For example, consistent enforcement of school rules and greater school support are associated with decreases in bullying and student-reported victimization (Gregory et al., 2010). Further, a positive school climate moderates the relationship between bullying and problematic outcomes for children, particularly with regard to homophobic teasing (Birkett et al., 2009). Children's perceptions of school climate also increase the likelihood of help-seeking behavior, with children who perceive a more supportive school climate being more likely to report bullying and threats of violence (Eliot, Cornell, Gregory, and Fan, 2010). One school factor that is linked particularly to the prevalence of school bullying is federally mandated student achievement assessments (Hazel, 2010; Juvonen et al., 2011). Although these assessments are designed to promote academic achievement, some research indicates that they have detrimental effects on the social-emotional climate of schools. Specifically, Hazel (2010) recently indicates that an increased emphasis on teaching certain academic skills that are related to student achievement assessments has left little room for meeting children's social-emotional and safety needs. Such a situation creates undue stress on both teachers and children and may prompt children to report a decreased sense of school safety. In turn, these factors lead to children's increased difficulty with focusing on academic work.

Given the serious implications of bullying for children's emotional and behavioral functioning, a number of interventions have been developed for classrooms in the United States to address bullying behavior. These interventions range from individually based interventions to school-wide interventions. One of the first bullying interventions was developed by Olweus in Norway (Olweus and Limber, 2010). The Olweus Bullying Prevention Program (OBPP) is based on the principles of adult warmth and interest in students, firm guidelines for behavior, consistent consequences for rule violations, and positive adult role models. Components of this program include conducting trainings with school staff, involving parents, posting and enforcing school-wide rules against bullying, supervising children's activities, ensuring that staff intervenes when bullying is observed, and helping to spread anti-bullying messages to the community. These components are implemented across school, classroom, individual, and community levels. This program has been studied less extensively in the United States but demonstrates some positive results (Olweus and Limber, 2010).

Several other interventions have been implemented in the United States, including the *Steps to Respect* (Frey, Hirschstein, Edstrom, and Snell, 2009) and the *Youth Matters* (Jenson, Dietrich, Brisson, Bender, and Powell, 2010) programs. Implementation of both of these programs is related to some declines in bullying behavior and victimization. Although these programs demonstrate some gains in appropriate behavior, their effects are moderate at best. In fact, a recent meta-analysis of bullying intervention programs reveals that the majority of intervention effects is relatively small and is not clinically significant (Merrell, Guelder, Ross, and Isava, 2008). Thus, it appears that more effective interventions are needed, particularly in the United States (Farrington and Ttofi, 2009).

In fact, a review of the literature suggests that a number of factors may be important for effective bullying interventions. One factor that consistently emerges as important is an increase in adult supervision and the provision of activities during unstructured free time (e.g., recess; Bauman, 2008; Bradshaw, Sawyer, and O'Brennan, 2009; Cunningham, Cunningham, Ratcliffe, and Vaillancourt, 2010; Farrington and Ttofi, 2009; Hughes et al., 2009). Further, it is important to train school personnel in how to recognize all types of bullying and how to effectively intervene once each type of bullying is recognized (Bradshaw et al., 2007). Children also should be provided with positive role models for appropriate behavior (Bauman, 2008), and schools should attempt to foster a positive school environment that promotes collaboration among peers and teachers (Cunningham et al., 2010; Flaspohler, Elfstrom, Vanderzee, and Sink, 2009). Thus, although bullying behavior is being recognized only recently as problematic, it is a highly prevalent form of problematic peer interaction that leads to a significant number of negative outcomes. Although researchers have proposed several interventions to address this behavior, no one intervention has proven to be highly successful in changing bullying behavior. It is likely that major changes in both schools and classrooms, in conjunction with support from families, will be needed in order to address this and other critical areas of social-emotional development.

## Working with Families

As already noted, the collaboration and mutual support that should occur between families and schools can be critical to children's academic achievement and social-emotional development. In fact, family-school relationships play a large role in the academic and social-emotional achievement of children (Jackson, Martin, and Stocklinski, 2004). According to Pianta and Walsh (1996), "School failure is at its core caused by an inability or an unwillingness to communicate- a relationship problem" (p. 24). The partnership between home and school is the central feature that moves school systems from a cycle of failure to a culture of success (Christenson and Sheridan, 2001). Given that families are the source of children's self-affirmation, children will likely feel alienated if their parents feel mistrust and detachment from their children's school and its staff (Jackson et al., 2004). By creating a comfortable and welcoming environment for both parents and school faculty, an effective collaboration can foster children's positive development (Jackson et al., 2004). Giving parents the opportunity to play a role in their children's education places a greater emphasis on individual children's needs, rather than employing a 'one-size-fits-all' approach.

According to Bronfenbrenner's (1979) Ecological Systems Theory, children are a part of an embedded social system that is made up of interrelated systems. In this theory, emphasis is placed on understanding children in the context of these interrelated systems. This theory is highly applicable to understanding the success of children in schools, given that family and school systems each play a substantial role in children's development, both independently and collaboratively (Christenson and Sheridan, 2001). Another theory, Epstein's (1987) Theory of Overlapping Spheres of Influence, similarly stresses the importance of shared responsibility between schools and families (Epstein, 1990). This theory recognizes that there are some practices that families and schools should carry out separately but that there are other practices that should be achieved collaboratively. With the utilization of these overlapping spheres, children can learn that their parents and their teachers are working together to help them reach specific goals (Epstein, 1990).

Christenson and Sheridan (2001) also propose that families and schools should be 'partners' that share a mutual goal. First, they suggest a student-focused philosophy in which families and teachers work together to enhance the academic, social-emotional, and behavioral aspects of all children. Second, they believe in a collective responsibility for educating and socializing children, wherein both parents and teachers are responsible for children's learning and progress. Next, they emphasize the quality of the relationship between families and schools as well as the importance of their ongoing connection and positive relationship. Finally, Christenson and Sheridan (2001) propose a preventative, solution-oriented focus that centers on creating environments that assist in learning and development.

Given the collaborative focus of each of these theories, beliefs or attitudes that families and schools hold about each other appear to be fundamental to the development of a mutually agreeable relationship. Often times, unhealthy connections result from the negative attitudes of families and schools toward each other. These negative attitudes may include considering adults' impressions of children from only one setting, failing to take the perspective of or to empathize with the other adults in family-school relationships, failing to view differences as potential strengths, failing to believe in a partnership orientation toward children's learning and development, and maintaining a blaming and labeling attitude. Such negative attitudes subsequently can cause barriers (Christenson and Sheridan, 2001). Thus, it seems crucial that both families and schools recognize the importance of the relationship that they enter when children enter school. In particular, it is essential that schools consider the uniqueness of each family and that both families and teachers are open to taking multiple perspectives (Christenson and Sheridan, 2001). With such a stance, both families and teachers must explore their roles and responsibilities and engage in self-assessment and self-reflection (Christenson and Sheridan, 2001). Further, the relationship between families and schools must be reciprocal in nature. In other words, it should be recognized that parents' involvement at their children's schools can improve the schools' climate and that the schools' climate can affect parents' involvement at their children's schools (Christenson and Sheridan, 2001). Thus, both families and schools must take a proactive approach to building the home-school relationship and for collaboratively fostering children's academic achievement and social-emotional development.

Such family involvement in schools can take several different forms. Jackson and colleagues (2004) suggest that such involvement can include parents and other family members supporting their children (i.e., parent/family involvement). Parents and other family members can attend or contribute to a variety of school activities, such as school performances, open house events, home-school organization meetings, report card conferences, sports events, chaperoning field trips, and volunteering in classrooms (Holowinsky, 1997; Jackson et al., 2004). Such activities can break down barriers between families and schools while creating an inviting, caring, and accepting environment. Of course, schools must offer such events and be open to parents' participation. Jackson and colleagues (2004) suggest that there are three basic steps for developing parent-school involvement. These steps include understanding parents' involvement at school, forming a parent team and building family membership on committees, and exploring barriers to family involvement and finding solutions.

Parents also may become involved through advocacy programs. Advocacy programs, such as the National Parent-Teacher Association (PTA), were established to provide a voice for children, to offer resources for parents and communities, and to advocate for the well-being of all children. Explicit in the goals of the PTA is bringing a closer relationship between families and schools so that parents and teachers can collaborate intelligently on behalf of children's education (National PTA, 2011). Other formal organizations and committees include the Parent-Teacher-Student Association (PTSA), school site council, and the Principal Advisory Committee (Christenson and Sheridan, 2001). The central purpose of each of these organizations is to allow families and schools to serve as co-decision makers, advocates, and advisors for children and to inform each other in a way that provides mutual support and enhances student learning (Christenson and Sheridan, 2001).

To ensure that parents and children are receiving the best services possible, legal policies also are available. Implicit under section 1118 of NCLB is the notion that parents' involvement in their children's education is crucial for children's academic achievement (U. S. Department of Education, 2011). Schools are responsible for coordinating and integrating parent involvement strategies to improve children's academic achievement and school performance and for organizing parent-teacher conferences, providing frequent reports on children's progress, and granting reasonable access to staff and services (U. S. Department of Education, 2011). In addition, the Family Engagement in Education Act builds statewide capacity for effective partnerships between families and schools and engages parents and the community in developing family participation in education (National PTA, 2011). Further, the Family Educational Rights and Privacy Act (FERPA) protects the rights of children's education records and gives parents the right to review, request amendments to, and release information about their children's education record (U. S. Department of Education, 2011). With regard to children with special needs, the Individuals with Disabilities Education Improvement Act of 2004 (IDEA, 2004) and Individualized Education Programs (IEP) both provide services to children with disabilities and place an emphasis on the importance of parents' involvement and their rights in this process (Sattler and Hoge, 2006; U. S. Department of Education, 2011).

According to the National Association of School Psychologists (2011), everyone benefits when parents and teachers work together. In particular, children attend school more regularly, have better behaviors, earn higher grades, and show more positive attitudes towards both themselves and their schools when parents and teachers work together (National Association of School Psychologists, 2011). Further, research suggests that partnerships between families and schools strengthens family relationships, improves schools, builds community support, and enhances children's academic achievement (National Education Association, 2011). Thus, meaningful communication between families and schools is the foundation upon which goals, expectations, and responsibilities are fulfilled, with mutual trust at the foundation (Christenson and Sheridan, 2001; Holowinsky, 1997; Margolis, 1999). With such meaningful communication, teachers can inform parents about children's progress, school programs, and curricula, while parents can report to schools information about their children's background, characteristics, and strengths (Christenson and Sheridan, 2001). Overall, families and schools need to work together to break down the barriers and ensure that children are getting the educational experiences that they deserve.

## RECOMMENDATIONS FOR THE FUTURE

As noted earlier, the intent of this chapter was to emphasize schools' role in children's academic achievement *as well as* children's social-emotional development. As already noted, schools unfortunately are facing many challenges in today's world, some of which are jeopardizing their role in fostering children's abilities. Clearly, issues with funding and accountability are changing the way in which schools are teaching our children. These issues appear to also have some effects on how boys (relative to girls) are adjusting to their current school settings, how well emotional and behavioral problems are being identified in current school settings, how children are treating their peers, and how schools and parents are working together (or not). Clearly, now that the focus of current school settings has shifted to high-stakes standardized assessment, there is less time to accommodate the individual needs of our children, resulting in a 'one-size-fits-all' approach. Unfortunately, this approach is unlikely to serve the majority of our children well.

As a result, other approaches are being discussed. For example, in approaching the future of our children in the context of their school experiences, Power, DuPaul, Shapiro, and Kazak (2003) argue that the services provided by schools should be integrated with other community-based resources and services, such as medical services, mental health services, and other services to facilitate positive relationships among family members and peers. Such a multicomponent approach would better address the needs of all children, including those who have special medical and mental health needs. It should be noted, however, that school professionals would need to set the tone and create the context for a mutually supportive family-school collaboration (Christenson and Sheridan, 2001). Although Power and Bartholomew (1987) describe five types of interaction styles (i.e., avoidant, competitive, merged, one-way, and collaborative) that may occur between schools and families, clearly a collaborative relationship would be of most benefit to our children.

Rork and McNeil (2008) also provide several suggestions for fostering effective school consultation. These suggestions including considering teachers' perspectives of different situation as well as considering the challenges that they are facing, building rapport with teachers, listening to teachers as they describe their concerns, and understanding the interventions that teachers have already tried. These suggestions also include parents sharing information about children's families with teachers, describing the special needs of their particular children, waiting for teachers to approach psychologists for help, showing enthusiasm for interventions while also acknowledging limitations, providing coaching and feedback, and tailoring consultations to the needs of teachers and particular situations. Clearly, all these suggestions focus on the collaboration between parents and teachers as well as other school professionals with a unique focus on each of our individual children, rather than utilizing a 'one-size-fits-all' approach with an emphasis on high-stakes standardized assessment. Perhaps we would all be best served by a return to the old adage, "It takes a village to raise a child". Perhaps then we can worry less about failing our children. Perhaps then we can focus more on fostering their academic achievement and their social-emotional learning and on watching them blossom as they enter the future. That is a fine vision indeed.

## REFERENCES

Altshuler, S. J., and Kopels, S. (2003). Advocating in schools for children with disabilities: What's the new IDEA? *Social Work, 48*, 320-329.

Altshuler, S. J., and Schmautz, T. (2006). No Hispanic student left behind: The consequences of "high stakes" testing. *Children and Schools, 28*, 5-16.

Ansary, N. S., and Luthar, S. S. (2009). Distress and academic achievement among adolescents of affluence: A study of externalizing and internalizing problem behaviors and school performance. *Development and Psychopathology, 21*, 319-341.

Arseneault, L., Bowes, L., and Shakoor, S. (2010). Bullying victimization in youths and mental health problems: 'Much ado about nothing?' *Psychological Medicine, 40,* 717-729.

Aviles, A. M., Anderson, T. R., and Davila, E. R. (2006) Child and adolescent social-emotional development within the context of school. *Child and Adolescent Mental Health, 11,* 32-39.

Banks, J. A., and Banks, C. A. (2007). *Multicultural education: Issues and perspectives (Sixth edition).* Hoboken, NJ: Wiley.

Barbarin, O. A. (2002). The view from research: Culture and ethnicity in social, emotional and academic development. *The Kauffman Early Education Exchange, 1,* 45–61.

Bauman, S. (2008). The role of elementary school counselors in reducing school bullying. *The Elementary School Journal, 108,* 362-375.

Bauman, S., and Del Rio, A. (2006). Preservice teachers' responses to bullying scenarios: Comparing physical, verbal, and relational bullying. *Journal of Educational Psychology, 98*, 219-231.

Bauman, S., Rigby, K., and Hoppa, K. (2008). U. S. teachers' and school counselors' strategies for handling school bullying incidents. *Educational Psychology, 28,* 837-856.

Beveridge, T. (2010). No Child Left Behind and fine arts classes. *Arts Education Policy Review, 111*, 4-7.

Birkett, M., Espelage, D. L., and Koenig, B. (2009). LGB and questioning students in schools: The moderating effects of homophobic bullying and school climate on negative outcomes. *Journal of Youth and Adolescence, 38,* 989-1000.

Blair, C. (2002). School readiness: Integrating cognition and emotion in a neurobiological conceptualization of children's functioning at school entry. *American Psychologist*, *57*, 111–127.

Blair, C., and Razza, R. P. (2007). Relating effortful control, executive function, and false belief understanding to emerging math and literacy ability in kindergarten. *Child Development*, *78*, 647–663.

Boyd, J., Barnett, W. S., Bodrova, E., Leong, D. J., Gomby, D., Robin, K., and Hustedt, J. T. (2005). *Promoting children's social and emotional development through preschool.* New Brunswick, NJ: National Institute for Early Education Research, Rutgers University.

Bouck, E. C. (2009). No Child Left Behind, the individuals with disabilities education act and functional curricula: A conflict of interest? *Education and Training in Developmental Disabilities, 44*, 3-13.

Bradley, R. H., Caldwell, B. M., Rock, S. L., Barnard, K. E., Gray, C., Hammond, M. A., Mitchell, S., Siegel, L., Ramey, C. T., Gottfried, A. W., and Johnson, D. L. (1989). Home environment and cognitive development in the first 3 years of life: A collaborative study involving six sites and three ethic groups in North America. *Developmental Psychology, 25*, 217-235.

Bradshaw, C. P, Sawyer, A. L., and O'Brennan, L. M. (2007). Bullying and peer victimization at school: Perceptual differences between students and school staff. *School Psychology Review, 36,* 361-382.

Bradshaw, C. P., Sawyer, A. L., and O'Brennan, L. M. (2009). A social disorganization perspective on bullying-related attitudes and behaviors:

The influence of school context. *American Journal of Community Psychology, 43,* 204-220.

Brick, B. (2005). Changing concepts of equal educational opportunity: A comparison of the views of Thomas Jefferson, Horace Mann, and John Dewey. *American Educational History Journal, 32,* 166-174.

Bronfenbrenner, U. (1979). Contexts of child rearing: Problems and prospects. *American Psychologist, 34,* 844-850.

Brooks-Gunn, J., Klebanov, P. K., Smith, J., Duncan, G. J., and Lee, K. (2003). The Black-White test score gap in young children: Contributions of test and family characteristics. *Applied Developmental Science, 7*, 239-252.

Buriel, R., Perez, W., DeMent, T., Chavez, V., and Moran, V. (1998). The relationship of language brokering to academic performance, biculturalism, and self-efficacy among Hispanic adolescents. *Hispanic Journal of Behavioral Sciences, 20,* 283-297.

Burns, T. G. (2010). Wechsler Individual Achievement Test-III: What is the 'gold standard' for measuring academic achievement? *Applied Neuropsychology, 17*, 234-236.

Byrnes, J. P. (2003). Factors predictive of mathematics achievement in White, Black, and Hispanic $12^{th}$ graders. *Journal of Educational Psychology, 95*, 316-326.

Campbell, S. (1995). Behavior problems in preschool children: A review of recent research. *Journal of Child Psychology and Psychiatry and Allied Disciplines*, *36*, 113–149.

Carbone-Lopez, K., Esbensen, F., and Brick, B. T. (2010). Correlates and consequences of peer victimization: Gender differences in direct and indirect forms of bullying. *Youth Violence and Juvenile Justice, 8,* 332-350.

Chamberlin, J. (2008). Lost boys. *Monitor on Psychology, June,* 44-46.

Christenson, S. L., and Sheridan, S. M. (2001). *Schools and families: Creating essential connections for learning.* New York: The Guilford Press.

Cohen, E., and Kaufmann, R. (2000). *Early childhood mental health consultation.* Rockville, MD: Center for Mental Health Services of the Substance Abuse and Mental Health Services Administration and the Georgetown University Child Development Center.

Coolahan, K., Fantuzzo, J., Mendez, J., and McDermott, P. (2000). Preschool peer interactions and readiness to learn: Relationships between classroom peer play and learning behaviors and conduct. *Journal of Educational Psychology, 92,* 458-465.

Council for Exceptional Children. (2003). *What every special educator must know: Ethics, standards, and guidelines for special educators (Fifth edition).* Arlington, VA: Council for Exceptional Children.

Cuban, L. (2003). Why have American public schools become an arm of the economy? In *Why is it so hard to get good schools?* (pp. 5-22). New York: Teachers College Press.

Cunningham, C. E., Cunningham, L. J., Ratcliffe, J., and Vaillancourt, T. (2010). A qualitative analysis of the bullying prevention and intervention recommendations of students in grades 5 to 8. *Journal of School Violence, 9,* 321-338.

DeAngelis, T. (2010). Social awareness + emotional skills = successful kids. *Monitor on Psychology, 41,* 46-49.

Deslatte, A., and Garcia, J. (2011, January 13). *Florida Senate president: Cuts in education funding are likely.* Retrieved from http://articles.orlandosentinel.com/2011-01-13/news/os-haridopolos-on-budget-20110112_1_tax-cuts-face-big-cuts-spending-cuts.

Dillon, S. (2006, March 26). Schools cut back subjects to push reading and math. *New York Times*, *1*, 1.

Dryfoos, J. G. (1997). The prevalence of problem behaviors: Implications for programs. In R. P. Weissberg, T. P. Gullotta, R. L. Hampton, B. A. Ryan, and G. R. Adams (Eds.), *Healthy children 2010: Enhancing children's wellness* (pp. 17-46). Thousand Oaks, CA: Sage.

Duckworth, A., and Seligman, M. E. (2006). Self-discipline gives girls the edge: Gender in self-discipline, grades, and achievement test scores. *Journal of Educational Psychology*, *98*, 198–208.

Duffy, M., Giordano, V. A., Farrell, J. B., Paneque, O. M., and Crump, G. B. (2008). No Child Left Behind: Values and research issues in high-stakes assessments. *Counseling and Values, 53,* 53-68.

Dukes, R., Stein, J. A., and Zane, J. I. (2009). Effect of relational bullying on attitudes, behavior, and injury among adolescent bullies, victims, and bully-victims. *The Social Science Journal, 46,* 671-688.

Eastin, D. (2008). Political report card. *Miller-McCune, June-July,* 20-25.

Eisenhart, M. A., and Finkel, E. (1998). *Women's science: Learning and succeeding from the margins*. Chicago: University of Chicago Press.

Elias, M. J. (2006). The connection between academic and social-emotional learning. In M. J. Elias and H. Arnold (Eds.), *The educator's guide to emotional intelligence and academic achievement* (pp 4-14). New Brunkswick, NJ: Collaborative for Academic, Social, and Emotional Learning (CASEL), Rutgers University.

Elias, M. J., and Arnold, H. (2006). *The educator's guide to emotional intelligence and academic achievement: Social-emotional learning in the classroom*. Thousand Oaks, CA: Corwin Press.

Eliot, M., Cornell, D., Gregory, A., and Fan, X. (2010). Supportive school climate and student willingness to seek help for bullying and threats of violence. *Journal of School Psychology, 48,* 533-553.

Elkind, D. (2001). *The hurried child: Growing up too fast too soon (Third edition)*. Cambridge, MA: Perseus.

Epstein, J. (1987). Toward a theory of family-school connections: Teacher practices and parent involvement. In K. Hurrelmann, F. Kaufmann, and F. Losel (Eds.), *Social intervention: Potentials and constraints* (pp. 121-136). Oxford, England: Walter De Gruyter.

Epstein, J. (1990). School and family connections: Theory, research, and implications for integrating sociologies of education and family. *Marriage and Family Review, 15*, 99-126.

Eveland-Sayers, B. M., Farley, R. S., Fuller, D. K., Morgan, D. W., and Caputo, J. L. (2009). Physical fitness and academic achievement in elementary school children. *Journal of Physical Activity and Health, 6*, 99-104.

Farrington, D. P., and Ttofi, M. (2009). How to reduce school bullying. *Victims and Offenders, 4,* 321-326.

Flaspohler, P. D., Elfstrom, J. L., Vanderzee, K. L., and Sink, H. E. (2009). Stand by me: The effects of peer and teacher support in mitigating the impact of bullying on quality of life. *Psychology in the Schools, 46,* 636-649.

Florence, M. D., Asbridge, M., and Veugelers, P. J. (2008). Diet quality and academic performance. *Journal of School Health, 78*, 209-215.

Freeman, C. (2004). *Trends in educational equity of girls and women*. Washington, DC: U.S. Department of Education, National Center for Education Statistics.

Frey, K. S., Hirschstein, M. K., Edstrom, L. V., and Snell, J. L. (2009). Observed reductions in school bullying, nonbullying aggression, and destructive bystander behavior: A longitudinal evaluation. *Journal of Educational Psychology, 101,* 466-681.

Frick, P. J., Kamphaus, R. W., Lahey, B. B., Loeber, R., Christ, M. G., Hart, E. L., and Tannenbaum, L. E. (1991). Academic underachievement and the disruptive behavior disorders. *Journal of Consulting and Clinical Psychology, 59*, 289-294.

Furnee, C. A., Groot, W., and van den Brink, H. M. (2008). The health effects of education: A meta-analysis. *European Journal of Public Health, 18*, 417-421.

Gandara, P., and Lopez, E. (1998). Hispanic students and college entrance exams: How much do they really matter? *Hispanic Journal of Behavioral Sciences, 20,* 17-38.

Gastic, B. (2008). School truancy and the disciplinary problems of bullying victims. *Educational Review, 60,* 391-404.

Glass, C. S., and Wegar, K. (2000). Teacher perceptions of the incidence and management of attention deficit hyperactivity disorder. *Education, 121,* 412-420.

Gonzalez, J. E., Nelson, J. R., Gutkin, T. B., and Shwery, C. S. (2004). Teacher resistance to school-based consultation with school psychologists: A survey of teacher perceptions. *Journal of Emotional and Behavioral Disorders, 12,* 30-37.

Gopaul-McNicol, S., Reid, G., and Wisdom, C. (1998). The psychoeducational assessment of Ebonics speakers: Issues and Challenges. *Journal of Negro Education, 67*, 16-27.

Greenberg, M. T., Weissberg, R .P., O'Brien, M. U., Zins, J. E., Fredericks, L., Resnik, H., and Elias, M. J. (2003). Enhancing school-based prevention and youth development through coordinated social, emotional, and academic learning. *American Psychologist, 58,* 466-474.

Gregory, A., Cornell, D., Fan, X., Sheras, P., Shih, T., and Huang, F. (2010). Authoritative school discipline: High school practices associated with lower bullying and victimization. *Journal of Educational Psychology, 102,* 483-496.

Griffith, G., and Scharmann, L. (2008). Initial impacts of No Child Left Behind on elementary science education. *Journal of Elementary Science Education, 20*, 35-48.

Gross-Loh, C. (2007, March-April). Give me that old-time recess. *Mothering,* 54-63.

Gutkin, T. B., and Hickman, J. A. (1990). The relationship of consultant, consultee, and organizational characteristics to consultee resistance to school-based consultation: An empirical analysis. *Journal of Educational and Psychological Consultation, 1,* 111-122.

Harmon, A. (2011, February 4). It may be a Sputnik moment, but science fairs are lagging. *The New York Times.* Retrieved from http://www.nytimes.com/2011/02/05/us/05science.html?nl=todaysheadlines.

Havey, J. M., Olson, J. M., McCormick, C., and Cates, G. L. (2005). Teachers' perceptions of the incidence and management of attention-deficit hyperactivity disorder. *Applied Neuropsychology, 12,* 120-127.

Hazel, C. (2010). Interactions between bullying and high-stakes testing at the elementary school level. *Journal of School Violence, 9,* 339-356.

Hess, F. M., and Petrilli, M. J. (2006). *No Child Left Behind.* New York: Peter Lang.

Hinduja, S., and Patchin, J. W. (2010). Bullying, cyberbullying, and suicide. *Archives of Suicide Research, 14,* 206-221.

Hinshaw, S. P. (1992). Externalizing behavior problems and academic underachievement in childhood and adolescence: Causal relationships and underlying mechanisms. *Psychological Bulletin, 111*, 127-155.

Hirsh-Pasek, K., and Golinkoff, R. M. (2003). *Einstein never used flash cards: How our children really learn – And why they need to play more and memorize less.* Emmaus, PA: Rodale Inc.

Hobbs, E. (2008, August 17). Will budget disaster mean kids learn less? *Orlando Sentinel.*

Holman, L. (1995). *Impact of ethnicity, class, and gender on achievement of border area students on a high-stakes examination.* East Lansing, MI: National Center for Research on Teaching Learning.

Holowinsky, I. Z. (1997). Partnership in education: Local, national, and international perspective. *School Psychology International, 18,* 61-79.

Hood, S. (1998). Culturally responsive performance-based assessment: Conceptual and psychometric considerations. *Journal of Negro Education, 67*, 187-196.

Howse, R. B., Calkins, S. D., Anastopoulos, A. D., Keane, S. P., and Shelton, T. L. (2003). Regulatory contributors to children's kindergarten achievement. *Early Education and Development, 14*, 101–119.

Hughes, P. P., Middleton, K. M., and Marshall, D. D. (2009). Students' perceptions of bullying in Oklahoma Public Schools. *Journal of School Violence, 8,* 216-232.

Jackson, S. (1994). Educating children in residential and foster care: An overview. *Oxford Review of Education, 20*, 267-279.

Jackson, S., Martin, N., and Stocklinski, J. (2004). Families as partners: Parent teams and parent/family involvement. In E. T. Joyner, M. Ben-Avie, and J. P. Comer (Eds.), *Transforming school leadership and management to support student learning and development* (pp. 105-126). Thousand Oaks, CA: Corwin Press.

Jencks, C., and Phillips, M. (1998). The Black-White test score gap: An introduction. In C. Jencks and M. Phillips (Eds.), *The Black-White test score gap* (pp. 1-54). Washington, DC: Brookings Institution.

Jenson, J. M., Dieterich, W. A., Brisson, D., Bender, K. A., and Powell, A. (2010). Preventing childhood bullying: Findings and lessons from the Denver Public Schools trial. *Research on Social Work Practice, 20,* 509-517.

Johnson, N., Oliff, P., and Koulish, J. (2008). Most states are cutting education. *Center on Budget and Policy Priorities.* Retrieved from http://www.cbpp.org/files/12-17-08sfp.pdf.

Johnson, N., Oliff, P., and Williams, E. (2011). An update on state budget cuts: At least 46 states have imposed cuts that hurt vulnerable residents and the economy. *Center on Budget and Policy Priorities*. Retrieved from http://www.cbpp.org/files/3-13-08sfp.pdf.

Juvonen, J., Wang, Y., and Espinoza, G. (2011). Bullying experiences and compromised academic performance across middle school grades. *The Journal of Early Adolescence, 31,* 152-173.

Krugman, P. (2011, February 27). Leaving children behind. *The New York Times.* Retrieved from http://www.nytimes.com/2011/02/28/opinion/28krugman.html.

Lee, J. (2006). *Tracking achievement gaps and assessing the impact of NCLB on the gaps: An in-depth look into national and state reading and math outcome trends.* Cambridge, MA: The Civil Rights Project at Harvard University.

Lee, V. E., and Burkam, D. (2002). *Inequality at the starting gate: Social background differences in achievement as children begin school.* Washington, DC: Economic Policy Institute.

Liljequist, L., and Renk, K. (2007). The relationships among teachers' perceptions of student behaviour, teachers' characteristics, and ratings of students' emotional and behavioural problems. *Educational Psychology: An International Journal of Experimental Educational Psychology, 27,* 557-571.

MacLeod, I. R., Jones, K. M., Somers, C. L., and Havey, J. M. (2001). An evaluation of the effectiveness of school-based behavioral consultation. *Journal of Educational and Psychological Consultation, 12,* 203-216.

Magnuson, K. (2007). Maternal education and children's academic achievement during middle childhood. *Developmental Psychology, 43*, 1497-1512.

Mandara, J., Varner, F., Greene, N., and Richman, S. (2009). Intergenerational family predictors of the Black-White achievement gap. *Journal of Educational Psychology, 101*, 867-878.

Margolis, H. (1999). Mediation for special education conflicts: An opportunity to improve family-school relationships. *Journal of Educational and Psychological Consultation, 10,* 91-100.

Mead, S. (2006). *The truth about boys and girls.* Retrieved from http://www.curriculum.org/secretariat/files/May17TruthBoysandGirls.pdf.

Meier, D., and Wood, G. (Eds.). (2004). *Many children left behind: How the No Child Left Behind Act is damaging our children and our schools.* Boston: Beacon Press.

Meijs, N., Cillessen, A., Scholte, R., Segers, E., and Spijkerman, R. (2010). Social intelligence and academic achievement as predictors of adolescent popularity. *Journal of Youth and Adolescence, 39*, 62-72.

Merrell, K. W., Guelder, B. A., Ross, S. W., and Isava, D. M. (2008). How effective are school bullying intervention programs? A meta-analysis of intervention research. *School Psychology Quarterly, 23,* 26-42.

Merrow, J. (2001). *Choosing excellence.* Lanham, MD: Scarecrow Press, Inc.

National Association of School Psychologists. (2011). Retrieved from http://www.nasponline.org/.

National Center for Education Statistics. (2002). *Dropout rates in the United States, 2000.* Washington, DC: U.S. Department of Education, Offices of Educational Research and Improvement.

National Commission on Excellence in Education. (1983*). A nation at risk: A report to the nation and secretary of education.* Washington, DC: U.S. Department of Education.

National Education Association, U.S. Department of Education Discrestionary Programs. (2011). *Impact of the House Continuing Resolution (H.R. 1) as Amended, FY 2011.* Retrieved from http://www.nea.org/assets/docs/ImpactofHouseFY11SpendingCuts.pdf.

National Institute for Mental Health (NIMH). (2000). *A good beginning: Sending America's children to school with the social and emotional competence they need to succeed.* The Child Mental Health Foundation and Agencies Network.

National Parent-Teacher Association. (2011). Retrieved from http://www.pta.org/.

Newcomb, A. F., Bukowski, W. M., and Pattee, L. (1993). Children's peer relations: A meta-analytic review of popular, rejected, neglected, controversial, and average sociometric status. *Psychological Bulletin, 113*, 99-128.

Newman, F. M., and Associates. (1996). *Authentic achievement: Restructuring schools for intellectual quality.* San Francisco: Jossey-Bass.

Noftle, E. E., and Robins, R. W. (2007). Personality predictors of academic outcomes: Big five correlates of GPA and SAT scores. *Journal of Personality and Social Psychology, 93*, 116-130.

Novick, R. M., and Isaacs, J. (2010). Telling is compelling: The impact of student reports of bullying on teacher intervention. *Educational Psychology, 30,* 283-296.

Office of Juvenile Justice and Delinquency Prevention. (2006). *Juvenile offenders and victims: 2006 national report.* Washington, DC: U. S. Department of Justice, Office of Justice Programs.

Olweus, D., and Limber, S. P. (2010). Bullying in school: Evaluation and dissemination of the Olweus Bullying Prevention Program. *American Journal of Orthopsychiatry, 80,* 124-134.

Onwuegbuzie, A. J., and Daly, C. E. (2001). Racial differences in IQ revisited: A synthesis of nearly a century of research. *Journal of Black Psychology, 27*, 209-220.

Osterman, K. F. (2000). Students' need for belonging in the school community. *Review of Educational Research, 70,* 323-367.

Pellegrini, A. D. (2002). Rough-and-tumble play from childhood through adolescence: Development and possible functions. In P. K. Smith and C. H. Hart (Eds.), *Blackwell handbook of child and social development* (pp. 437-453). Malden, MA: Blackwell.

Pellegrini, A. D., and Bohn, C. M. (2005). The role of recess in children's cognitive performance and school adjustment. *Educational Researcher, 34,* 13-19.

Perry, D. F., Dunne, M. C., McFadden, L., and Campbell, D. (2008). Reducing the risk for preschool expulsion: Mental health consultation for young children with challenging behaviors. *Journal of Child and Family Studies, 17,* 44-54.

Peterson, W., and Rothstein, R. (2010). Let's do the numbers: Department of Education's "Race to the Top" program offers only a muddled path to the finish line. *Economic Policy Institute Briefing Paper, 263,* 1-10.

Pianta, R., and Walsh, D. B. (1996). *High-risk children in schools: Constructing sustaining relationships.* New York: Routledge.

Power, T. J., and Bartholomew, K. (1987). Family-school relationship patterns: An ecological perspective. *School Psychology Review, 16,* 498-512.

Power, T. J., DuPaul, G. J., Shapiro, E. S., and Kazak, A. E. (2003). *Promoting children's health: Integrating school, family, and community.* New York: The Guilford Press.

Pullen, P. L. (2004). *Brighter beginnings for teachers.* Lanham, MD: Scarecrow Education.

Rapport, M. D. (2005). Commentary: School-based observations of children at school: Promise with prudence. *School Psychology Review, 34,* 537-542.

Raver, C. C. (2002). Emotions matter: Making the case for the role of young children's emotional development for early school readiness. *Social Policy Report, 16,* 13-19.

Raver, C. C., and Knitzer, J. (2002). *Ready to enter: What research tells policymakers about strategies to promote social and emotional school readiness among three- and four-year-old children.* New York, NY: National Center for Children in Poverty, Mailman School of Public Health, Columbia University.

Reinke, W. M., Herman, K. C., Petras, H., and Ialongo, N. S. (2008). Empirically derived subtypes of child academic and behavior problems: Co-occurrence and distal outcomes. *Journal of Abnormal Child Psychology, 36,* 759-770.

Rescorla, L. A., Achenbach, T. M., Ginzburg, S., Ivanova, M., Dumenci, L., Almqvist, F., Bathiche, M., Bilenberg, N., Bird, H., Domuta, A., Erol, N., Fombonne, E., Fonseca, A., Frigerio, A., Kanbayashi, Y., Lambert, M. C., Liu, X., Leung, P., Minaei, A., Roussos, A., Simsek, Z., Weintraub, S., Weisz, J., Wolanczyk, T., Zubrick, S. R., Zukauskiene, R., and Verhulst, F. (2007). Consistency of teacher-reported problems for students in 21 countries. *School Psychology Review, 36,* 91-110.

Rescorla, L.A., Achenbach, T.A., Ivanova, M, Dumenci, L., Almqvist, Bilenberg, N, Bird, H, Chen, W., Dobrean, A., Dopfner, M., Erol, N., Fombonne, E., Fonseca, A., Frigerio, Greitins, H., Hannesdottir, H., Kanbayashi, Y., Lambert, M. C., Larsson, B., Leung, P., Liu, X., Minaei, A, Mulatu, M.S., Novik, T.S., Oh, K., Roussos, A., Sawyer, M., Simsek, Z, Steinhausen, H., Weintraub, S., Weisz, J., Metzke, C.W., Wolanczyk, T., Yang, H., Zilber, N., Zukauskiene, R., and Verhulst, F. (2007). Behavioral and emotional problems reported by parents of children ages 6 to 16 in 31 societies. *Journal of Emotional and Behavioral Disorders, 15,* 130-142.

Rimm-Kaufman, S. E., Pianta, R. C., and Cox, M. J. (2000). Teacher's judgments of problems in the transition to kindergarten. *Early Childhood Research Quarterly, 15,* 147-166.

Rork, K. E., and McNeil, C. B. (2008). A behavioral model of school consultation. *The Behavior Therapist, 31,* 69, 71-73.

Roth, P., Bevier, C., Bobko, P., Switzer, F., and Tyler, P. (2001). Ethnic group differences in cognitive ability in employment and educational settings: A meta-analysis. *Personnel Psychology, 54*, 297-330.

Sadker, M., and Sadker, D. (1994). *Failing at fairness: How America's schools cheat girls*. New York: Macmillan.

Sattler, J. M., and Hoge, R. D. (2006). *Assessment of children: Behavioral, social, and clinical foundations (Fifth edition).* California: Jerome M. Sattler, Publisher, Inc.

Schwartz, D., Hopmeyer Gorman, A., Duong, M. T., and Nakamoto, J. (2008). Peer relationships and academic achievement as interacting predictors of depressive symptoms during middle childhood. *Journal of Abnormal Psychology, 117*, 289-299.

Shaw, J. M. (2005). Getting things right at the classroom level. In J. L. Herman and E. H. Haertel (Eds.), *Uses and misuses of data for educational accountability and improvement* (pp. 340-357). Malden, MA: National Society for the Study of Education/Blackwell.

Shilts, M., Lamp, C., Horowitz, M., and Townsend, M. S. (2009). Pilot study: EatFit impacts sixth graders' academic performance on academic achievement of mathematics and English education standards. *Journal of Nutrition Education and Behavior, 41,* 127-131.

Siegel, J. (1999). Stigmatized and standardized varieties in the classroom: Interference or separation? *TESOL Quarterly, 33*, 701-728.

Silverman, I. W. (2003). Gender differences in delay of gratification: A meta-analysis. *Sex Roles*, *49*, 451–463.

Sommers, C. H. (2000). *The war against boys: How misguided feminism is harming our young men*. New York: Simon and Schuster.

Steinberg, L. (1996). *Beyond the classroom: Why school reform has failed and what parents need to do*. New York: Touchstone.

Stetson, R., Stetson, E. G., and Sattler, J. M. (2001). Assessment of academic achievement. In J. M. Sattler (Ed.), *Assessment of children: Cognitive Applications* (pp. 576-609). La Mesa, CA: John Sattler, Publisher, Inc.

Sunderman, G. E., Kim, J., and Orfield, G. (2005). *NCLB meets school realities: Lessons from the field*. Thousand Oaks, CA: Corwin Press.

Swearer, S. M., Turner, R. K., Givens, J. E., and Pollack, W. S. (2008). "You're so gay!": Do different forms of bullying matter for adolescent males? *School Psychology Review, 37,* 160-173.

Tanner, D. E., Newbold, B. L., and Johnson, D. B. (2003). *Academic achievement as a drop out predictor.* Project report. Fresno, CA: California State University. (ERIC Document Reproduction Service No. ED 478 173).

Taras, H. (2005). Nutrition and student performance at school. *Journal of School Health, 75*, 199-213.

Thomas, J. Y., and Brady, K. P. (2005). The elementary and secondary school act at 40: Equity, accountability, and the evolving federal role in public education. *Review of Research in Education, 29*, 51-67.

Thompson, R., and Happold, C. (2002). The roots of school readiness in social and emotional development. *The Kauffman Early Education Exchange, 1,* 8-29.

Trautwein, U., Ludtke, O., Robers, B. W., Schnyder, I., and Niggli, A. (2009). Difference forces, same consequences: Conscientiousness and competence beliefs are independent predictors of academic effort and achievement. *Journal of Personality and Social Psychology, 97*, 1115-1128.

U. S. Department of Education. (2011). Retrieved from http://www.ed.gov/.

Varjas, K., Henrich, C. C., and Meyers, J. (2009). Urban middle school students' perceptions of bullying, cyberbullying, and school safety. *Journal of School Violence, 8,* 159-176.

Villegas, A. M., and Lucas, T. (2007). The culturally responsive teacher. *Educational Leadership, 64*, 28-33.

Wang, J., Iannotti, R. J., and Nansel, T. R. (2009). School bullying among adolescents in the United States: Physical, verbal, relational, and cyber. *Journal of Adolescent Health, 45,* 368-375.

Weaver-Hightower, M. (2003). The "boy turn" in research on gender and education. *Review of Educational Research, 73*, 471–498.

Weber, D. (2011, January 18). Seminole teachers to get bonuses instead of raises. *Orlando Sentinel.* Retrieved from http://articles.orlando sentinel.com/2011-01-18/news/os-seminole-teachers-pay-011911-20110118_1_seminole-teachers-sanford-teachers-teacher-pay-talks.

Wentzel, K. R., and Asher, S. (1995). Academic lives of neglected, rejected, popular, and controversial children. *Child Development, 66*, 754–763.

Whitted, K. (2011). Understanding how social and emotional skill deficits contribute to school failure. *Preventing School Failure, 55,* 10-16.

Wienke Totura, C. M., Green, A. E., Karver, M. S., and Gesten, E. L. (2009). Multiple informants in the assessment of psychological, behavioral, and academic correlates of bullying and victimization in middle school. *Journal of Adolescence, 32,* 193-211.

Wittberg, R. A., Cottrell, L. A., Davis, C. L., and Northrup, K. L. (2010). Aerobic fitness thresholds associated with fifth grade academic achievement. *American Journal of Health Education, 41*, 284-291.

Wittberg, R. A., Northrup, K. L., and Cottrel, L. (2009). Children's physical fitness and academic performance. *American Journal of Health Education. 40*, 30-36.

Woodcock, R. W., McGrew, K. S., and Mather, N. (2001). *Woodcock-Johnson Tests of Achievement.* Itasca, IL: Riverside Publishing.

Zins, J. E., and Elias, M. J. (2006). Social and emotional learning. In G. G. Bear and K. M. Minke (Eds.), *Children's needs III: Development, prevention, and intervention* (pp. 1-14). Bethesda, Maryland: National Association of School Psychologists.

In: Child and School Psychology
Editors: M. Haines et al., pp. 51-83
ISBN: 978-1-61470-801-8


*Chapter 2*

# RECEPTION GRADE TEACHERS' PERCEPTIONS OF LANGUAGE AND LITERACY DEVELOPMENT, SPEECH-LANGUAGE PATHOLOGISTS, AND LANGUAGE INTERVENTION

*Nicole Randall and Munyane Mophosho*
School of Human and Community Development
University of the Witwatersrand, Johannesburg, South Africa

## INTRODUCTION AND RATIONALE

Before most children enter school, his/her primary experience with language is in the oral mode (Gambrell, 2004; Nation and Snowling, 2004). Once the child arrives at school, language becomes more abstract, as it becomes the vehicle of learning (Nelson, 1985). Without adequate language skills, learning in a classroom setting becomes difficult. Westby (1985) explains that on the oral-to-literate continuum, school activities are at the extreme literate end of the spectrum. This means the child is required to comprehend and convey information that is disconnected from his/her own experience. Abadiano and Turner (2005, pp. 60) state, "To become a skilled reader, children need a rich language and conceptual knowledge base, a broad and deep vocabulary, and verbal reasoning abilities to understand messages that are conveyed through print." It is evident from this statement that language development must precede literacy development. Children must be proficient in oral language before they can learn to read and write (Catts and Fey, 1999; Roth, Speece, and Cooper, 2002). It should be noted that children with language impairments are at high risk for literacy disabilities (Lewis, O'Donnell, Freebairn, and Taylor, 1998). Abadiano and Turner (2005), also highlight the importance of preschool attendance as a predictor of literacy success later in the school career.

Once the child enters the school environment, the classroom teacher often has the first opportunity to identify children with language impairments (Owens, 2004). Language impairments in children are often accompanied by difficulties in learning to read and write (Schuele, 2004). It is often easier for a classroom teacher to identify a literacy disability, as this is directly within their scope of teaching, than for them to identify language impairment. It is not uncommon for speech-language therapists (SLTs) to have to alert classroom teachers to the features that signal possible language impairment in a child (Owens, 2004).

In their training, it is obvious that teachers do not receive as much input on language development as SLTs do. Thus it follows that it would be more difficult for them to identify language difficulties, as opposed to literacy deficits, in a child in their classroom. This may be the case even when language and literacy difficulties occur together, as they often do (Schuele, 2004). Teachers are generally more skilled in identifying literacy impairments, as they are more familiar with the norms for literacy in children than SLTs are.

In past years, early childhood educators in South Africa did not have to be registered, qualified or certified to open a pre-grade school, kindergarten or crèche (Jacobs, 2001). There have been recent publications concerning Early Childhood Development (ECD) and the registration and qualification of teachers in this field (Early Childhood Development Policy, 2001). Qualification and certification for teachers of young children in this country will soon become enforced. Numerous teachers, before this policy was introduced, could not be called much more than "caregivers" (National Professional Teachers Organization of SA, 2001-2005). This implies that many of the teachers of Reception Grade, as we now know it, though possibly having had many years of experience in caring for children, may not have had much input or education concerning the development of language and literacy as well as the roles and responsibilities of SLTs. This may have bearing on their ability to recognize the value of language development for literacy and other academic learning.

The purpose of this study will be to look into whether there is a need in the Johannesburg area for more teacher education, specifically concerning when to refer children for speech-language therapy and the importance of knowledge of language and literacy development. The National Professional Teachers Organization of South Africa (NAPTOSA) has made it apparent that the White Paper on Grade R Teachers is not clear in terms of the training Early Childhood Educators should receive or have received concerning language development, as well as the Language of Learning and Teaching (National Professional Teachers Organization of SA, 2001-2005).

Butler (1999) details how the role of the speech-language pathologist has changed from being more focused on the oral speech-language disorders to, more recently, including literacy. Teachers, particularly those of the early grades, have always handled the domain of literacy. There is now a call for speech-language therapists and early childhood educators to work together in a collaborative effort to address both professionals' areas of expertise, as very often, children who are affected by difficulties are affected in both areas (Norris and Damico, 1990). Moyer (2001) has researched the "kindergarten", as preschool settings, and has found a need to once again make it "child-centered". Making a Grade 0 or K classroom "child-centered" would definitely mean a collaborative effort between teacher and speech-language therapist, in cases where language and literacy development is involved. This would address the child's learning as a whole and not separate out the language and literacy aspects of learning.

This overlap between the two professions (early childhood education and speech-language therapy) makes it necessary for each to have knowledge concerning the scope of the other's profession. The SLT is equipped with knowledge concerning the identification and remediation of speech-language impairments; teachers on the other hand, know each child in their classroom and are aware of how to use large and small group interaction for efficient teaching. Classroom teachers should be educated in the scope and practice of SLTs and vice versa, as each is in possession of unique skills that can be used to help each other and the child with language and literacy impairments. In short, there should be a move towards a more collaborative approach, in which there is role sharing and role release (Ehren and Ehren, 2001).

Various barriers occur in the negotiation of the roles of both the teacher and the SLT in the classroom. These barriers include both individual inhibitors and system inhibitors.

Individual inhibitors include the fear of change, the desire for autonomy, narrow role definition resulting in lack of training, and the traditional perception of roles on both the SLT and the teachers' parts (Ehren and Ehren, 2001). System inhibitors include those imposed by current policies and practices. The culture of the school, caseload and time limitations and policies limiting opportunities can become barriers that stand in the way of effective collaboration between teachers and other professionals, more specifically SLTs. Action can be taken to reduce and eliminate these barriers by identifying them and being prepared to assume new and expanded roles (Ehren and Ehren, 2001). Through effective communication and enlisting the support of one another, collaborative efforts can be very productive. This requires effort and negotiation but can be achieved over time and has been shown to be effective for the students concerned (Roth and Baden, 2001).

The ideal place to educate classroom teachers and SLTs regarding each other's professions would be in the settings in which they are educated. This research aims to gather information regarding what teachers know concerning the roles of SLTs, as well as their knowledge of language and literacy development. This will give insight into whether teachers are adequately equipped to identify children with language and literacy impairments and make the correct referrals. Furthermore, this will reveal whether there is a gap in the education of teachers concerning language development that should be addressed in the future.

In the original research paper (Shaughnessy and Sanger, 2005) a survey study examined the perceptions of 484 kindergarten teachers concerning language and literacy development, the roles and responsibilities of SLTs and teacher-delivered interventions in the classroom.

This was done, in one midwestern state of the United States of America, and both qualitative and quantitative measures were undertaken. Using a thirty-six item survey questionnaire, the original researchers found that the majority of the respondents had had professional training and appreciated the importance of language development, could identify some signals associated with atypical language development in young children and were supportive of language development in their classrooms. They also found that the participants had an accurate awareness of the expertise of the speech-language therapist. In general, findings suggested teachers were positive about their shared roles and welcomed opportunities to collaborate with SLTs in areas of language and literacy (Shaughnessy and Sanger, 2005).

This research hypothesizes that South African teachers are insufficiently trained to identify and refer children with language disorders appropriately.

# METHOD

## 1. Aims of the Research

This research aims to investigate the willingness and ability of Early Childhood Educators, more specifically Grade R teachers in Johannesburg, to understand and deal with the language development of the children they teach. According to the Education White Paper 5 on Early Childhood Education (2001), policies were put in place to make sure that early childhood educators are required to have knowledge concerning language development, as this is important to the development of reading and writing skills (Gambrell, 2004). The research is a replication of a study that was completed in the Midwestern United States by Shaughnessy and Sanger (2005).

Until the White Paper 5 was released recently in South Africa, the view could be taken which is similar to the American study, that this country has teachers that are insufficiently prepared to identify and refer children with language difficulties. The implications are that if children are not identified for language disorders early in their schooling that they will not receive appropriate remediation. Not identifying these early also has implications for later school performance.

Sub-aims of the research include investigating the need for SLTs to market their profession more thoroughly at the level at which teachers receive *their* education.

This research has previously not been explored in a South African setting.

## 2. Research Design

A 36-item survey was developed by the original researchers (Shaughnessy and Sanger, 2005) for use in this study (See Appendix 1). The questionnaire was modified for use in a South African context with the permission of the original researchers. The data obtained from the use of this questionnaire were analyzed both quantitatively and qualitatively.

## 3. Research Ethics

In order to send questionnaires to government schools in the study, permission of the Gauteng Education Department was requested for the government schools. Permission to perform the research at government schools in the area was granted pending the permission of the principal of each school to be used. Attached to the questionnaires was an information letter to the principal of each school, requesting permission to give the questionnaires to the Grade R teachers in that school. If the principal declined to allow the researcher to continue, that school was left out of the final sample. In terms of the private schools, protocol involved liaising with principals of each school and requesting permission in the same way as had been done with the government schools. Following these measures, the teachers themselves were invited to participate in the study. Those teachers who chose not to participate were left out of the final sample. Teachers, principals and the Gauteng Education Department were informed that the results of the study would be available to them. They were also informed that there would be no direct benefit to them by their participation in the study.

## 4. Sample

### *4.1. Sampling Method*

The sample was chosen for convenience purposes due to the time constraints placed on the researcher. The sample was composed from a list of schools within the Johannesburg North East area that fit the criterion of having Grade R teachers at the school.

### *4.2. Sampling Procedure*

A list of schools was compiled by the researched cataloguing over one hundred schools within the designated geographical area in which the study was to take place. Each school was telephonically contacted to ascertain whether they had Grade R teachers teaching at the school. Forty-four schools currently had at least one Grade R teacher teaching at the school. The names of those schools were submitted to the Gauteng Education Department for approval and permission was granted by them to begin the research at those schools pending the permission of each school's principal. The principal of each school was then telephonically contacted to request permission to conduct research within his/her school. Thirty-one principals gave permission for research to be conducted. Each Grade R teacher at each of the thirty-one schools was then invited to participate in the study. The final count of individuals who chose to participate in the research was thirty-one teachers. The final count of schools participating in the research was twenty-two. It should be noted that the period of data collection coincided with a national public servants' strike followed by school holidays, during which time, teachers at government institutions were not available for participation. This made the collection of data difficult and is the reason for a smaller sample size than the researchers had hoped for.

### *4.3. Description of Participants*

The sample consisted of thirty-one Grade R teachers, working in the Johannesburg North East area. Demographic information regarding gender, ethnicity, highest degree earned, year of completion of highest degree, years employed in education, and additional certifications are detailed in Table 1.

## 5. Materials

The questionnaire used in the study is a slightly modified version of the one used in the original survey (Shaughnessy and Sanger, 2005). The modifications that have been made have not changed the content of the questionnaire at all; they have only made the questionnaire more appropriate for use in a South African context. The researcher received permission from the authors of the original study to use and modify the questionnaire. The questionnaire was developed by the original researchers (Shaughnessy and Sanger, 2005) for the purpose of the original study. They also handed the drafted items for the questionnaire were to experts in survey research and professionals in language development for revision and approval. This process was repeated until the final version was deemed acceptable for use in the study. The participation of the experts conferred with guards against any content validity issues. The questionnaire was found to be appropriate on the whole for the purpose of this replication study. Items that were not suitable for use in a South African context were modified slightly so as to make them more acceptable. It should be noted, however, that the content of the items was not adjusted and remains as it was in the original questionnaire. Questions 3f, 10 and 16 have been slightly modified to make them appropriate to a South African context. The word "digraph" in Question 3f was omitted. In Question 10, the phrases "primary grades" and "elementary school" were changed to "foundation phase" and "senior phase". Lastly, the word "eligible" in Question 16 was replaced with "a candidate".

**Table 1. Summary of Demographic Information and Professional Development of Survey Participants (N=31)**

| Demographic Factor | Category | n | % |
|---|---|---|---|
| Gender | Female | 30 | 96.7 |
| | Male | 1 | 3.33 |
| Ethnicity | White | 17 | 54.84 |
| | Black | 2 | 6.45 |
| | Coloured | 1 | 3.23 |
| Highest Degree Earned | H Dip Ed | 5 | 16.13 |
| | Diploma | 9 | 29.03 |
| | B Ed | 6 | 19.35 |
| | Montessori | 1 | 3.23 |
| | Other | 4 | 12.90 |
| | None | 1 | 3.23 |
| Year of highest degree completion | Before 1960 | 0 | 0 |
| | 1961-1970 | 2 | 6.45 |
| | 1971-1980 | 6 | 19.35 |
| | 1981-1990 | 4 | 12.90 |
| | 1991-2000 | 6 | 19.35 |
| | Since 2000 | 10 | 32.26 |
| Years employed in education | 0-5 | 10 | 32.26 |
| | 6-10 | 5 | 16.13 |
| | 11-15 | 3 | 9.68 |
| | 16-20 | 4 | 12.90 |
| | 21-25 | 4 | 12.90 |
| | 26-30 | 2 | 6.45 |
| | More than 30 | 3 | 9.68 |
| Certifications | Early Childhood | 21 | 67.74 |
| | Special Education | 2 | 6.45 |
| | Senior Phase Education | 3 | 9.68 |
| | Reading Specialist | 1 | 3.23 |
| | Other | 1 | 3.23 |

Note. N=31. Totals for individual categories may not equal the total number surveyed. Some participants did not respond to every item and more than one option could be selected in the category "Certifications".

The questionnaire itself contains three main sections. The first section consists of seven items pertaining to demographic information of the participant, three items concerning the professional training of the teacher and two items regarding the teachers' experience in working with SLTs. These include whether they are currently or have previously worked with children who receive speech therapy as well as the models of service delivery most commonly used (a pull out system or therapy given within the classroom environment). This section utilizes a tick-all-that-apply and fill-in format. The second section contains forty-one Likert-type items, respectively. The Likert-type items are rated on a five-point scale ranging from *strongly disagree* to *strongly agree*, with the midpoint reflecting *neither agree nor disagree*. The response category for this section was the circling of one point on the five-point scale. The content of the items in section two focus on the perceptions of the teachers, pertaining to language and literacy development in children, the roles and responsibilities of SLTs, and teacher-administered interventions. The items have been phrased in such a way that they either reflect or contradict typical children's language and literacy development, specifically in the first five years of life. For example, questionnaire item number 1 (section two) states, "Children develop language by observing how others use and respond to language." All items have been based on reputable sources, such as the American Speech-Language-Hearing Association's Guidelines for the Roles and Responsibilities of School-Based Speech Language Pathologists (1999). Section three consists of two open-ended items. Subjects were invited to comment regarding their experience in teaching language and literacy to children, and about the scope of the survey.

## 6. Procedures

### *6.1. Data Collection*

The researcher collected data by hand-delivering the following to each teacher, or school, in the case of more than one teacher at a particular school:

- A written request for participation, to be signed by the principal An information letter, setting out the purpose, scope and procedure of the study as well as including details of the researcher. Consent was requested in this document.
- Copies of the modified questionnaire to be filled out by each Grade R teacher at the school.

Initially, the researcher attempted to deliver and collect the questionnaires to a particular school in the same day, giving participants a reasonable amount of time (three to four hours) to complete the questionnaire. This was intended to enlist the co-operation of participants and to allow the researcher to adhere to strict time constraints. However, it became clear that teachers were unable to complete the questionnaire on the day it was delivered. It should be noted that the data was collected at the end of the school term and teachers were found to be extremely busy with the assessment and reports of the children in their classes. Most teachers required a few days to complete the questionnaire due to the sheer volume of their workloads. Also, many schools were involved in a national public servants' strike and so were not available to participate on some days. Following this discovery, questionnaires and consent forms were either collected a few days after having been delivered or faxed back to the researcher.

## 6.2. Data Analysis

Data was analyzed quantitatively to tabulate the demographic information and to calculate means on the Likert-type questions and qualitatively to extract themes from the open-ended questions. In some questionnaires, the participants did not answer all the questions. This meant that there were variations in the sample sizes for each question. Data were calculated on the total number of questionnaires completed, that is, thirty-one (N=31) and "no responses" were considered in the calculations. Descriptive analysis was utilized to analyze responses regarding background information and professional training.

Overall means and standard deviations were calculated for each of the Likert-type items. The criteria set up by the original researchers were used to indicate agreement or disagreement (Shaughnessy and Sanger, 2004). *Strongly agree* was represented as the number 1 with *strongly disagree* represented as the number 5. Means from 1.00 to 2.49 were interpreted as agreement with the questionnaire item; means from 2.50 to 3.50 were interpreted as a neutral response and means from 3.51 to 5.00 were interpreted as disagreement with the statement in the questionnaire. These were tabulated and appear in Table 2.

Qualitative analysis also took place in order to evaluate the two open-ended questions in section three. Twelve of the thirty-one participants responded to the questions in this section. It is thought that this was due to the fact that this section required the most thought and time to answer, and teachers were too busy to do so. Similar responses were grouped together and themes or general ideas were extracted. These themes were categorized so as to eliminate repetition. The non-repetitive statements were termed *significant statements* and were used to develop core themes.

**Table 2. Grade R Teachers' responses to Likert-type Items on Language and Literacy Development, Roles and Responsibilities of SLTs and Teacher-Delivered Interventions**

| | Item | Response | | | | | |
|---|---|---|---|---|---|---|---|
| | | SA/A | | Uncertain | | D/SD | |
| | | M | StdD | M | StdD | M | StdD |
| | Language and Literacy Development | | | | | | |
| 1. | Children develop their language by observing how others use and respond to language | 2.00 | 1.00 | | | | |
| 2. | Children develop language through conversations | 1.00 | 1.00 | | | | |
| 3a. | Children whose language is developing as predicted understand more words than they use in daily conversations. | 1.70 | 0.60 | | | | |
| 3b. | Children whose language is developing as predicted understand and use basic conversational skills, such as initiating conversation, establishing and maintaining eye contact, taking turns, and staying on topic. | 1.90 | 0.80 | | | | |
| 3c. | Children whose language is developing as predicted understand and use most forms of plurals, possessives, and past tense verb endings. | 2.40 | 0.90 | | | | |
| 3d. | Children whose language is developing as predicted understand and respond appropriately to most forms of questions (c.g. who, what, where, when, why, how). | 2.00 | 0.80 | | | | |
| 3e. | Children whose language is developing as predicted understand and use figurative language, such as similes, metaphors, and idioms. | 2.90 | 1.10 | | | | |
| 3g. | Children whose language is developing as predicted recognize which spoken words rhyme. | 2.30 | 0.90 | | | | |

**Table 2. (Continued)**

| Item | | Response | | | | | |
|---|---|---|---|---|---|---|---|
| | | SA/A | | Uncertain | | D/SD | |
| | | M | StdD | M | StdD | M | StdD |
| 3h. | Children whose language is developing as predicted recognize which spoken words have the same beginning sound. | 2.20 | 0.70 | | | | |
| 4. | Children with weak phonemic awareness are likely to have difficulty learning to read. | 2.00 | 1.00 | | | | |
| 5. | Children whose language is not developing as predicted are more likely to have difficulty learning to read. | 2.00 | 1.00 | | | | |
| 6. | Experience with environmental print, books, and other literacy materials helps children develop concepts and skills necessary for reading and writing. | 1.00 | 1.00 | | | | |
| 12. | Children who have difficulty learning to read should be assessed for language problems. | 2.20 | 0.80 | | | | |
| 16. | Children whose language is not developing as predicted will be a candidate for speech-language services. | 2.10 | 0.90 | | | | |
| 22. | Professional training in language development is important for teachers of young children. | 1.90 | 0.90 | | | | |
| 3f. | Children whose language is developing as predicted correctly pronounce all consonant, and vowel sounds. | | | 2.80 | 1.00 | | |
| 8. | Children must receive formal instruction in all literacy skills and concepts in order to read and write. | | | 3.00 | 1.00 | | |
| 9. | Children whose language is developing as predicted may decode words they cannot comprehend. | | | 3.00 | 1.00 | | |

| Item | | Response | | | | | |
|---|---|---|---|---|---|---|---|
| | | SA/A | | Uncertain | | D/SD | |
| | | M | StdD | M | StdD | M | StdD |
| 10. | Children who do not master reading skills during foundation phase are likely to be reading at grade level by the end of senior phase. | | | 3.20 | 1.00 | | |
| 11. | Children who do not master reading skills during foundation phase are likely to have reading problems throughout their lives. | | | 3.00 | 1.00 | | |
| 13. | Children whose written work is not grammatically correct should be assessed for language problems. | | | 2.80 | 1.90 | | |
| 14. | Children who easily converse with others will easily understand classroom lessons and directions. | | | 2.50 | 1.20 | | |
| 15. | Language does not develop as predicted in approximately 5% to 8% of young children. | | | 2.50 | 0.70 | | |
| 7. | Once children begin to read and write, their oral language skills do not develop further. | | | | | 4.00 | 1.00 |
| 19. | Teachers do not need to understand language development in order to teach children to read or write. | | | | | 3.90 | 1.00 |
| Roles and Responsibilities of SLTs | | | | | | | |
| 17a. | Speech-language therapists provide effective services for children whose language is not developing as predicted. | 1.65 | 0.61 | | | | |
| 17b. | Speech-language therapists provide effective services for children who have difficulty learning to read or write. | 1.96 | 0.75 | | | | |

**Table 2. (Continued)**

| Item | | Response | | | | | | |
|---|---|---|---|---|---|---|---|---|
| | | SA/A | | Uncertain | D/SD | | | |
| | | M | StdD | | M | StdD | M | StdD |
| 17c. | Speech-language therapists provide classroom teachers with effective suggestions for meeting the needs of students whose language is not developing as predicted. | | 2.14 | 0.78 | | | | |
| 17d. | Speech-language therapists provide classroom teachers with effective suggestions for meeting the needs of students who have difficulty reading or writing. | | 2.38 | 0.76 | | | | |
| 18a. | Classroom teachers and speech-language therapists should share responsibility for serving children with oral language problems. | | 1.77 | 0.43 | | | | |
| 18b. | Classroom teachers and speech-language therapists should share responsibility for serving children who have difficulty reading or writing. | | 2.00 | 0.59 | | | | |
| 20. | Speech-language services are delivered effectively through a variety of models. | | 2.30 | 0.60 | | | | |
| 21. | Direct service from the speech-language therapist is necessary for students verified for therapy. | | 2.00 | 0.80 | | | | |
| Teacher-Delivered Interventions | | | | | | | | |
| 23a. | Teachers should support children's language development by modelling the correct pronunciation of a word the child says incorrectly, then having the child repeat that word correctly. | | 2.19 | 1.17 | | | | |

| Item | | Response | | | | | |
|---|---|---|---|---|---|---|---|
| | | SA/A | | Uncertain | | D/SD | |
| | | M | StdD | M | StdD | M | StdD |
| 23b. | Teachers should support children's language development by restating the child's idea in correct grammatical form and having the child repeat it. | 2.19 | 1.05 | | | | |
| 23c. | Teachers should support children's language development by giving the child extra time to respond to questions. | 1.74 | 0.44 | | | | |
| 23e. | Teachers should support children's language development by rephrasing complex statements in simpler form. | 1.90 | 0.65 | | | | |
| 23g. | Teachers should support children's language development by giving one direction at a time. | 2.26 | 0.93 | | | | |
| 23h. | Teachers should support children's language development by explaining new vocabulary before reading a text. | 1.94 | 0.89 | | | | |
| 23d. | Teachers should support children's language development by asking yes/no questions instead of open-ended ones. | | | | | 3.47 | 1.25 |
| 23f. | Teachers should support children's language development by coaching the child in conversations with peers. | | | | | 2.80 | 1.37 |

*Key*: SA=Strongly Agree; A=Agree; D=Disagree; SD=Strongly Disagree; M=Mean; StdD=Standard Deviation.

**Table 3. Themes Extracted from Open-Ended Questions Regarding Participant's Experiences Teaching Language and Literacy to Young Children**

| Theme | | Significant Statements | Participants responding to theme | | Descriptive Statements | |
|---|---|---|---|---|---|---|
| | | | *n* | % | *n* | % |
| Learner characteristics and experience with learners | ♦ | Language development is incidental | 7 | 58.33 | 14 | 58.33 |
| | ♦ | Reading development is incidental | | | | |
| | ♦ | Having the correct attitude to reading is important | | | | |
| | ♦ | Second language learners learn English fast but they are difficult to teach | | | | |
| | ♦ | Learners language and literacy seems to be getting worse every year | | | | |
| | ♦ | There is poor modelling at home | | | | |
| | ♦ | Parents are in denial - they start trying to fix problems once the child is in Grade 1 which is too late in my opinion | | | | |
| Experience with SLTs | ♦ | SLTs are necessary | 5 | 41.67 | 6 | 25.00 |
| | ♦ | SLTs are better one-on-one, they battle with large class control | | | | |
| | ♦ | We need Black SLTs who speak African languages | | | | |
| | ♦ | Speech therapists differ in ability | | | | |
| | ♦ | SLTs provide essential/critical services and are well trained | | | | |
| | ♦ | SLTs are effective especially for auditory processing | | | | |
| Request for information and training | ♦ | What phonics programmes do you recommend? | 4 | 33.33 | 4 | 16.67 |
| | ♦ | Teachers need more training in language development | | | | |
| | ♦ | I am only teaching rhyming and reading stories | | | | |
| | ♦ | We do not do formal reading/writing in Grade R | | | | |

Table 3 lists the core themes extracted from the open-ended questions, along with frequency data, detailing the frequency with which each statement occurred among the total comments.

## RESULTS

The results obtained from the questionnaires are presented below beginning with demographic information, teachers' experiences with SLTs and speech therapy service delivery models, and continuing with results in the areas of language and literacy development, roles and responsibilities of SLTs, and teacher-delivered interventions.

Demographic professional training information of the participants has been presented in Table 1. The sample sizes for each question vary as not all questions were answered on the questionnaires, as well as the format of some questions being "tick-all-that-apply". Findings indicated that 96.7% (*n*=30) of participants were women and 3.23% (*n*=1) were men, with all participants responding. Many participants identified themselves as White (54.84%, *n*=17), 6.45% as Black (*n*=2) and one participant described herself as being Coloured (3.23%, *n*=1). Close to one third of participants did not respond to this question (32.36%, *n*=10). The lack of response in this question is thought to be related to the fact that this question could be viewed as being racially charged, and given the racial history of this country it is understandable that some participants would not want to provide their ethnicity. In terms of years of employment in education, 32.26% of teachers have been teaching for five years or less (*n*=10), with a range who have been teaching for between six and thirty years.

Roughly one third of participants had completed their highest degree since 2000, that is, in the past seven years (32.26%, *n*=10), with 15% of teachers possessing non-teaching degrees, including training such as Bachelor of Commerce and Bachelor of Social Work. 3.23% (*n*=1) of the participants in the sample reported having no qualification. Two thirds of the participants (67.74%, *n*=21) had obtained either a teaching degree or a diploma.

Two thirds of participants had obtained a certificate in Early Childhood Development (67.74%, *n*=21) and 35.48% (*n*=11) had taken at least one undergraduate course in language development. Only 9.68% of participants had at least one postgraduate degree in the area of language development (*n*=3). One third of respondents reported attending employer-provided in-service training in the area of language (32.26%, *n*=10). In the area of literacy, more than 40% of respondents reported having taken at least one undergraduate course (41.94%, $n$=13); much fewer participants had obtained at least one postgraduate degree in literacy (12.90%, $n$=4). Over 45% of participants reported having attended employer provided in-service training in the area of literacy (45.16%, $n$=14).

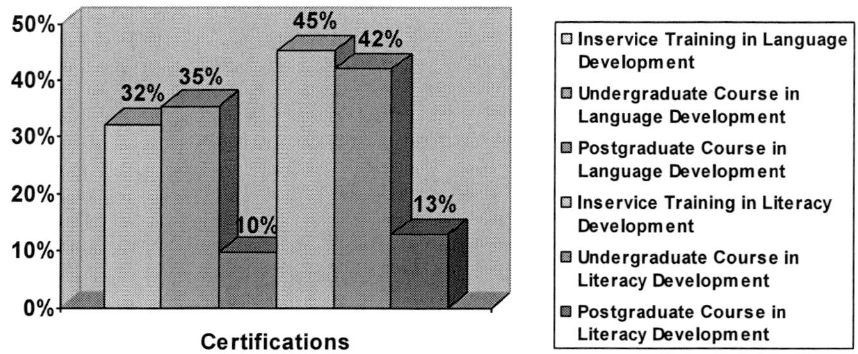


Figure 1. Professional Development in Areas of Language and Literacy.

About 45% of participants were currently working with learners receiving speech therapy services (45.16%, $n$=14), one quarter of participants had previously worked with such learners (25.81%, $n$=8). 61.29% ($n$=19) of participants were currently and had previously worked with such students (See Figure 2). The questionnaire gave eight possible types of interactions with clinicians and participants were required to tick all that they had experienced.

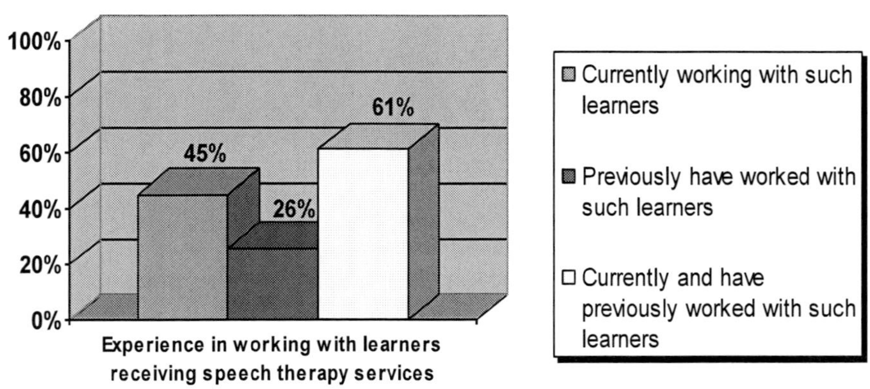


Figure 2. Teachers' Experience in Working with Learners Receiving Speech Therapy Services.

35.48% ($n$=11) of the participants indicated that an SLT currently pulled learners out of the classroom for therapy and 25.81% ($n$=8) indicated that they had experienced such a model. Only 3.23% ($n$=1) of respondents was currently and had previously used a collaborative model of service delivery, that is, team teaching. Other options listed, which were reported less frequently included shared planning followed by the teacher or a paraprofessional delivering therapy, a paraprofessional providing services within the classroom setting, and a paraprofessional providing services outside the classroom (See Figure 3).

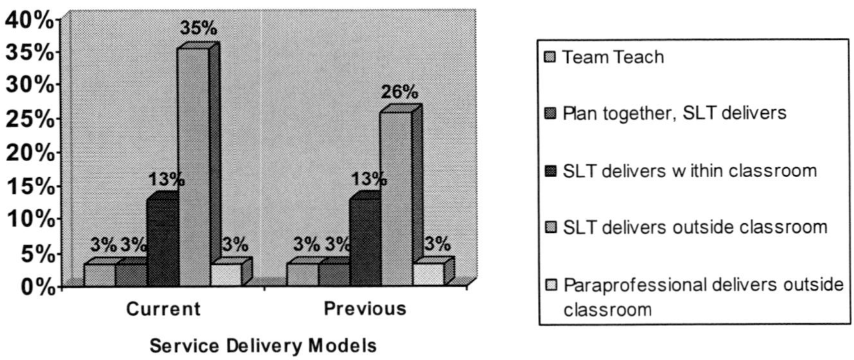


Figure 3. Current and Previously Used Service Delivery Models Used by Grade R Teachers.

Results on the Likert-type questions are listed below. They are grouped according to the three themes, that is, perceptions of language and literacy development, roles and responsibilities of speech language therapists, and teacher-delivered language intervention. Table 2 shows a summary of the means and standard deviations (descriptive statistics) for these items.

### *Perceptions of Language and Literacy Development*

Twenty-two questions in the questionnaire related to teachers' perceptions of language and literacy development. Mean findings illustrated that Grade R teachers agreed with 15 items relevant to the language and literacy development of Grade R learners. The following are the questions relating to language and literacy development with which participants were in agreement: Questions 1, 2, 3a, 3b, 3c, 3d, 3e, 3g, 3h, 4, 5, 6, 12, 16, and 22 (the actual questions can be found in Table 2). Uncertainty among respondents was noted on eight items. These were: Questions 3f, 8, 9, 10, 11, 13, 14, and 15.

Additionally, respondents disagreed with two items about language and literacy development. These were Questions 7, and 19.

### *Roles and Responsibilities of SLTs*

Eight questionnaire items pertained to the roles and responsibilities of the SLT. Respondents indicated agreement with all eight items: Questions 17a, 17b, 17c, 17d, 18a, 18b, 20, and 21.

### *Language Interventions*

The questionnaire contained eight items regarding the ways teachers should support learners' language development. Respondents agreed with six statements indicating various ways teachers should give this support: Questions 23a, 23b, 23c, 23e, 23g, and 23h. Respondents were uncertain with two of the statements relating to language interventions: Questions 23d, and 23f.

### *Findings from the Open-Ended Questions*

A total of twenty-four statements provided by twelve participants were analyzed and are represented in Table 3. Themes which emerged from the comments given by participants in reference to their experiences in teaching young children included (a) comments concerning learners' characteristics and experiences, (b) comments concerning experience with SLTs, and (c) comments requesting information and additional training in the area of language development.

Descriptive statistics showed that of the twelve participants who commented, more than half did so in the area of learners' characteristics and experience (58.33%). Five out of twelve (41.67%) teachers commented regarding their experience with SLTs, and one third (33.33%, or four 4 out of 12) made some kind of request for more information regarding language development and made comments indicating their awareness of a lack of training. These statistics are shown in Figure 4.

When comparing the number and percentage of statements above to the themes of the statements, similar information was obtained. Most of the comments (58.33%, or 14 out of 24) referred to learners' characteristics and experience with learners. Just below one quarter (25%, or six out of 24) of the comments were about teachers' experience with SLTs and one quarter (16.67%, or four out of 24) were a request for more information or training in the area of language development. An example of this was one teacher's comment stating, "Teachers need more training in language development."

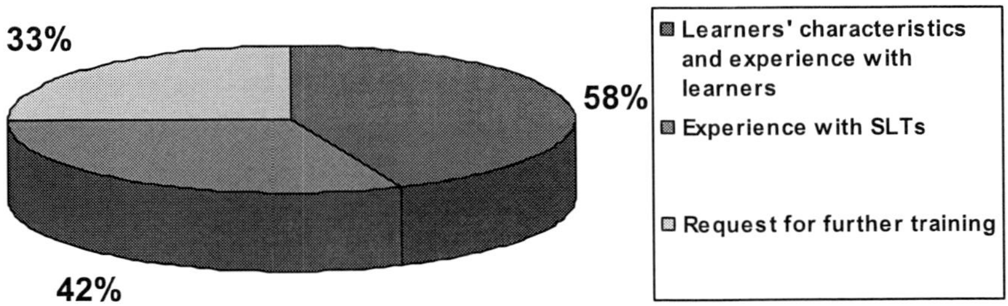


Figure 4. Themes extracted from comments made by participants.

# Discussion and Conclusion

Language and literacy are undeniably interconnected (Abadiano and Turner, 2005; Catts and Fey, 1999; Roth, Speece, and Cooper, 2002). However, there has been limited research to describe the way early childhood educators consider language and literacy. The response rate of questionnaires returned (70.45% of schools who qualified to participate) indicated that there is an interest in this area. This is seems to be the case, especially as the research was conducted during a period of increased pressure upon the teachers involved due to strike action, as well as the research being conducted at the end of a school term.

Even though this study was important in gathering information on the subject of collaboration between teachers and SLTs, the sample size and homogeneity amongst participants somewhat limits the possibility of generalization across South African populations. It should also be noted that responses are subjective and that this may be a limitation of the study, particularly in the interpretation of the results. However, findings from this research offer some groundwork from which future research can be explored.

Close to two thirds of participants (61.29%) indicated that their current and previous experience of service delivery is one in which the SLT pulls the child out of the classroom for therapy. A much smaller number indicated use of a collaborative model (6.46%, current and previous). This was notable in light of the fact that most teachers agreed with a Likert-type statement that speech therapy services could be delivered through a variety of models (see Table 2, Question 20). Participants also responded that direct service from an SLT is necessary for learners requiring therapy (see Table 2, Question 21). This brings to light a contradiction that may be due to participants' previous experiences with SLTs impacting on their responses. There is much research that addresses the need to use more inclusive service delivery models (Horn, Lieber, Sandall, and Schwartz, 2001; So and Lam, 2000). Curriculum-based intervention could be employed by SLTs in an attempt to make speech therapy more inclusive. These findings are not unequivocal and further research will have to be undertaken concerning models of speech-language therapy service delivery in South Africa. Further research into teachers' perceptions of collaborative consultation and its effectiveness as a model of service delivery will need to be undertaken.

## Language and Literacy Development

Findings showed that teachers might have more knowledge pertaining to language and literacy development than has been thought in the past (Fillmore and Snow, 2000). Teachers agreed with statements about the use of plurals, possessives, wh-type questions, rhyming, and phonological awareness in language development. Also, teachers' responses showed that they are well informed when it comes to referring a child for assessment based on difficulty in learning to read (See Table 2, Question 12). This is in line with research that has been published in the past (Tager-Flusberg, 1993). However, teachers' were unsure whether a child whose writing is grammatically incorrect should be referred for a language assessment. This shows a gap in the knowledge of teachers and could be related to possible barriers forming in collaborative efforts, that is, that teachers are not comfortable with SLTs addressing written language in their scope of practice.

Uncertainty was expressed for eight items on the questionnaire. The content of these items included the consequences of children not mastering the skill of reading in the foundation phase. It was clear from the responses given that teachers are not certain whether a child will "catch up later" if he/she does not master reading by the end of foundation phase. They were also unsure whether this would lead to problems with reading throughout life. Previous research describes the consequences of failure to master reading in the early grades (Share, and Leiken, 2004; Moats, 2001). The literature suggests that children who have difficulty learning to read in the early grades are often below grade level throughout their schooling careers. Findings indicating that participants are not sure about these statements may be linked to the idea that Grade R teachers might not see that child's development once he/she has left Grade R and moves on through foundation and senior grades. Inferring from the results found in the study, teachers need more instruction regarding the consequences of reading difficulty in the early grades. This could be done by including it in the curriculum at teacher training facilities or by SLTs approaching qualified teachers with information in this area.

Teachers were also unsure of the ability of typically developing children to pronounce all sounds. This may be related to individual variability of the learners in each class and is in agreement with literature. Most children in Grade R are five to six years old. At this age articulation of some sounds are not yet fully developed, so children who are not pronouncing all sounds correctly may still be considered to be within normal limits (Bleile, 1996).

Uncertainty was expressed about whether children who converse easily with others will easily understand classroom lessons and directions. This could be related to individual variability and the question being somewhat ambiguous. It could have been interpreted in different ways, for example, children who converse easily with highly effective communication partners may still have difficulty in the classroom, whereas children who communicate effectively with peers may not have difficulty in the classroom.

Participants disagreed with two statements in the questionnaire, which, considering the wording of the statements, have encouraging implications. Responses to both statements were consistent with current literature indicating that teachers perceive that children's oral language skills do continue to develop once they begin to read and write. This suggests that teachers understand the relationship between oral and written language. Also, teachers are in agreement that they need an understanding of language to be able to teach children to read and write. This is consistent with statements made in the open-ended section in which teachers commented concerning the need for further training and information regarding language. This shows that teachers comprehend the importance of their own knowledge of language development and that they may even be aware of a gap in their education.

## Roles and Responsibilities of SLTs

Teachers were in agreement with all statements with reference to the roles and responsibilities of SLTs.

Teachers indicated that SLTs provide effective services for children learning to read and write. This response is contradictory to one discussed above, which denotes that teachers are uncertain whether to refer a child with writing problems to a speech-language therapist. The response is also incongruous with a statements made that SLTs provide effective suggestions for classroom teachers in meeting the needs of learners who have difficulty reading or writing, and that SLTs and teachers should share responsibility for providing services to such learners. Further research into this area will be needed to ascertain the true perceptions of teachers in this regard. It may also point to the need that teachers need more information about the link between oral and written language, in other words, language and literacy development.

## Teacher-Delivered Interventions

Participants responses to most items of this nature (six out of eight) were in agreement with statements specifying that teachers themselves should support children's language development using modeling, rephrasing of complex statements, simplification of instructions, and vocabulary expansion and development. Furthermore, teachers made it clear that asking questions in a more open-ended manner is preferable to asking yes/no questions. These findings show that teachers are somewhat willing to share roles in attending to the needs of children who have language difficulties.

## Findings from the Open-Ended Questions

Twenty-four statements from twelve participants revealed their experiences in teaching young children, their beliefs, perspectives and concerns.

As noted in Table 3, the primary theme running through answers to the open-ended questions was based on the teachers' experiences with learners' as well as learner characteristics. A topic that came through strongly was that of having to work with second language English learners. This is a reality in South Africa and leads to the next topic that emerged within this theme, that of "poor modeling" at home.

Teachers believed that development of language in the children they teach could not be accurately assessed unless in the child's home language. One teacher commented that there is a need for SLTs who speak African languages. This is a promising finding as it opens up a discussion concerning speech therapy in languages other than English in South Africa.

Most teachers who commented about their own experience with SLTs had positive comments, such as "SLTs are necessary", SLTs are effective/critical and are well-trained", and "SLTs are effective, especially for auditory processing". This shows potential for future attempts at collaborative consultation. It confirms that teachers have had mostly positive experiences with SLTs, which would make it easier for them to co-function with them than if they had had negative experiences. There were a small number of negative comments including "SLTs differ in ability" and "SLTs are better one-on-one, they battle with large class control".

These statements, though negative in comparison to others could still be seen as constructive.

Furthermore, teachers have commented requesting further information and training in the area of language development. This is a positive factor as it shows awareness of a gap in their training and a willingness to learn.

Clinical implications for SLTs include providing information to teachers, both at the level of their training as well as in collaboration with them. The implications of teachers being less informed than they could be are that they may not be referring children who would benefit from speech-language therapy to SLTs. It is important that SLTs market their scope of practice to teachers at all times.

Limitations of this study include the fact that no pilot study was conducted. This could have saved the researcher time and allowed for improved efficacy. Clinical implications are that by teachers and SLTs working together, children with language and literacy difficulties can be identified and remediated earlier, in addition to addressing the problems of more than one child at a time, in a classroom situation.

In conclusion, Grade R teachers have a general awareness of language and literacy development with the exception of the consequences of not mastering reading in the early grades. They are also responsive in terms of delivering services to learners with language problems.

In terms of collaborative consultation, it seems as though there are the beginnings of awareness and willingness to participate in such models. However, there are still many teachers who are unsure regarding the effectiveness of speech-language therapy for children who have difficulty with reading and writing. In general, their eagerness to obtain more information and training is positive. Although, the findings of this study have been positive, it is not feasible to generalize to other South African cities or provinces and this could be called a limitation of this study. Further research in this area is necessary.

# Appendix 1

Survey on Young Children's Language and Literacy Development

This study is interested in your perceptions of young children's language and literacy development. There are no right or wrong answers. Please respond to every item, and feel free to add any comments you wish. Thank you for your participation.

Please tick (√) or fill in the most appropriate response for each of these items.

Highest degree earned:

____ BA (Education)

____ MA (Education)

____ PhD (Education)

____ Other: please describe here

Year of completion of highest degree:

____ Before 1960

____ 1961-1970

____ 1971-1980

____ 1981-1990

____ 1991-2000

____ Since 2000

Gender

____ Female

____ Male

Ethnicity: Please describe here

__________________________

Number of years employed in education

____ 0-5 years

____ 6-10 years

____ 11-15 years

____ 16-20 years

____ 21-25 years

____ 26-30 years

____ more than 30 years

Type of school:

____Government School

____Private School

Method of education:

____Traditional

____Montessori

____Other: please specify

Please tick (√) all responses that apply for each of these items.

Certifications/Endorsements

____ Early childhood

____ Preschool disabilities

____ Special Education

____ Speech-Language Therapist

____ Senior Phase Education

____ Reading specialist

____ Other: please describe here

Professional preparation focused on *literacy* development during early childhood

____Undergraduate course(s)

how many? ____

____ Postgraduate course(s)

how many? ____

____ Inservice training provided by employer

approximate number of hours ____

____ None

Professional preparation focused on *language* development during early childhood

____ Undergraduate course(s)

how many? ____

____ Postgraduate course(s)

how many? ____

____ Inservice training provided by employer

approximate number of hours ____

____ None

Experience with students receiving speech-language therapy at school

____ Currently have such student(s)

____ Previously have had such student(s)

____ Have not worked with such student(s)

Please tick (√) all responses that apply for each of these items.

Experience with speech-language therapists (SLTs)

____ *Currently* work with SLT to meet objectives for student(s)

____*Previously* have worked with SLT to meet objectives for student(s)

____ Team teach

____ Plan together, SLT delivers services

____ Plan together, teacher delivers services

____ Plan together, paraprofessional delivers services (e.g. class assistant)

____ SLT delivers services to student(s) within classroom

____ SLT delivers services to student(s) outside of classroom

____ Paraprofessional delivers services to student(s) within classroom

____ Paraprofessional delivers services to student(s) outside of classroom

Please indicate the strength of your agreement or disagreement with each statement that follows as a generalization about typical Grade R students. If you feel that you do not have sufficient information or experience to provide an opinion about a particular statement, circle "N". Please circle only one response for each statement.

SA = Strongly A gree D = Disagree
A = Agree SD = Strongly Disagree
N = Neither agree nor disagree

| | SA | A | N | D | SD |
|---|---|---|---|---|---|
| 1. Children develop their language by observing how others use and respond to language | SA | A | N | D | SD |
| 2. Children develop language through conversations | SA | A | N | D | SD |
| 3. Children whose language is developing as predicted | | | | | |
| a. understand more words than they use in daily conversations. | SA | A | N | D | SD |
| b. understand and use basic conversational skills, such as initiating conversation, establishing and maintaining eye contact, taking turns, and staying on topic. | SA | A | N | D | SD |
| c. understand and use most forms of plurals, possessives, and past tense verb endings. | SA | A | N | D | SD |
| d. understand and respond appropriately to most forms of questions (e.g. who, what, where, when, why, how). | SA | A | N | D | SD |
| e. understand and use figurative language, such as similes, metaphors, and idioms. | SA | A | N | D | SD |
| f. correctly pronounce all consonant, and vowel sounds. | SA | A | N | D | SD |
| g. recognize which spoken words rhyme. | SA | A | N | D | SD |
| 4. Children with weak phonemic awareness are likely to have difficulty learning to read. | SA | A | N | D | SD |
| 5. Children whose language is not developing as predicted are more likely to have difficulty learning to read. | SA | A | N | D | SD |
| 6. Experience with environmental print, books, and other literacy materials helps children develop concepts and skills necessary for reading and writing. | SA | A | N | D | SD |
| 7. Once children begin to read and write, their oral language skills do not develop further. | SA | A | N | D | SD |
| 8. Children must receive formal instruction in all literacy skills and concepts in order to read and write. | SA | A | N | D | SD |

| | | | | | |
|---|---|---|---|---|---|
| 9. Children whose language is developing as predicted may decode words they cannot comprehend. | SA | A | N | D | SD |
| 10. Children who do not master reading skills during foundation phase are likely to be reading at grade level by the end of senior phase. | SA | A | N | D | SD |
| 11. Children who do not master reading skills during foundation phase are likely to have reading problems throughout their lives. | SA | A | N | D | SD |
| 12. Children who have difficulty learning to read should be assessed for language problems. | SA | A | N | D | SD |
| 13. Children whose written work is not grammatically correct should be assessed for language problems. | SA | A | N | D | SD |
| 14. Children who easily converse with others will easily understand classroom lessons and directions. | SA | S | N | D | SD |
| 15. Language does not develop as predicted in approximately 5% to 8% of young children. | SA | S | N | D | SD |
| 16. Children whose language is not developing as predicted will be a candidate for speech-language services. | SA | S | N | D | SD |

Please indicate the strength of your agreement or disagreement with each statement that follows as a generalization about speech-language therapists and speech-language therapy. If you feel that you do not have sufficient information or experience to provide an opinion about a particular statement, circle "N". Please circle only one response for each statement.

SA = Strongly A gree D = Disagree
A = Agree SD = Strongly Disagree
N = Neither agree nor disagree

17. Speech-language therapists provide
    a. effective services for children whose language is not developing as predicted. SA A N D SD
    b. effective services for children who have difficulty learning to read or write. SA A N D SD
    c. classroom teachers with effective suggestions for meeting the needs of students whose language is not developing as predicted. SA A N D SD
    d. classroom teachers with effective suggestions for meeting the needs of students who have difficulty reading or writing. SA A N D SD
18. Classroom teachers and speech-language therapists should share responsibility for serving children
    a. with oral language problems SA A N D SD
    b. who have difficulty reading or writing SA A N D SD
19. Teachers do not need to understand language development in order to teach children to read or write. SA A N D SD
20. Speech-language services are delivered effectively through a variety of models. SA A N D SD
21. Direct service from the speech-language therapist is necessary for students verified for therapy. SA A N D SD
22. Professional training in language development is important for teachers of young children. SA A N D SD
23. Teachers should support children's language development by
    a. modeling the correct pronunciation of a word the child says incorrectly, then having the child repeat that word correctly. SA A N D SD
    b. restating the child's idea in correct grammatical form and having the child repeat it. SA A N D SD
    c. giving the child extra time to respond to questions. SA A N D SD
    d. asking yes/no questions instead of open-ended ones. SA A N D SD
    e. rephrasing complex statements in simpler form. SA A N D SD
    f. coaching the child in conversations with peers. SA A N D SD
    g. giving one direction at a time. SA A N D SD
    h. explaining new vocabulary before reading a text. SA A N D SD

Thank you for participating in this study. Your comments are welcome, here or on a separate page,

- about your experiences teaching young children language and literacy.
- about the scope of this survey Are there other topics that should have been included? Are any of these items irrelevant?

## REFERENCES

Abadiano, H. R., and Turner, J. (2005). Early literacy and developmentally appropriate practice: Closing the achievement gap. *New England Reading Association Journal, 41*(2), 60-67.

American Speech-Language-Hearing Association (1999). *Guidelines for the roles and responsibilities of the school based speech-language pathologist.* Rockville, MD.

Asmal, K. (2001). Education White Paper 5 on Early Childhood Education: Meeting the challenge of Early Childhood Development in South Africa. Department of Education: Pretoria.

Berninger, V.W., Vermeulen, K, Abbott, R.D. and McCutchen, D. (2003). Comparison of three approaches to supplementary reading instruction for low-achieving second-grade readers. *Language, Speech and Hearing Services in Schools, 34*(2), 101-118.

Bleile, K.M. (1996). *Articulation and Phonological Disorders: A Book of Exercises.* (2nd ed.). San Diego: Singular Publishing Group.

Bodrova, E., Leong, D.J. and Paynter, D.E. (1999). Literacy standards for preschool learners. *Educational Leadership, 57*(2), 42-47.

Butler, K.G. (1999). From oracy to literacy: Changing clinical perceptions. *Topics in Language Disorders, 20*(1), 14-33.

Catts, H.W., and Fey, M.E. (1999). Language Bases of Reading and Reading Disabilities: Evidence from a Longitudinal Investigation. *Scientific Studies of Reading, 3*(4), 331-361.

Ehren, B.J., and Ehren, T.C. (2001). New or Expanded Literacy Roles for Speech-Language Pathologists: Making It Happen in the Schools. *Seminars in Speech and Language, 22*(3), 233-243.

Fillmore, L.W., and Snow, C.E. (2000). *What teachers need to know about language.* Washington, DC: Department of Education

Gambrell, L. (2004). Exploring the connection between oral language and early reading. *The Reading Teacher, 57*(5), 490-492.

Horn, E., Lieber, J., Sandall, S., and Schwartz, I. (2001). Embedded learning opportunities as an instructional strategy for supporting children's learning in inclusive programs. In M. Otrosky and S. Sandall (Eds.), *Teaching strategies: What to do to support young children's development* (Monograph series no. 3; pp. 59-70). Denver, Colorado: Division for Early Childhood of the Council for Exceptional Children.

Jacobs, I.P. (2001). Early Childhood Development Policy. *Department of Education Policy Register, section 3 (2) of the Education Policy Act.* Pretoria.

Lance, D.M., Beverly, B.L., Evans, L.H. and McCollough, K.C. (2003). Addressing literacy: Effective methods for reading instruction. *Communication Disorders Quarterly, 25*(1), 5-12.

Lewis, B.A., O'Donnell, B., Freebairn, L.A., and Taylor, (1998). Spoken Language and written expression – Interplay of delays. *American Journal of Speech-Language Pathology, 7*(3), 77-84.

Moats, L.C. (2001) When older students can't read. *Educational Leadership, 58*(6), 36-40.

Moyer, J. (2001). The Child-Centered Kindergarten. *Childhood Education, 77*(3), 161-167.

Nation, K., and Snowling, M.J. (2004). Beyond Phonological Skills: Broader language skills contribute to the development of reading. *Journal of Research in Reading, 27*(4), 342-356.

National Professional Teachers Organization of SA, (2001-2005), NAPTOSA'S Comments on the White Paper for Early Childhood Development. Retrieved February 6, 2006, from http://www.naptosa.org.za

Nelson, N.W. (1985). Teachers talk and children listen – Fostering a better match. In C. Simon (Ed.), *Communication skills and classroom success: Assessment of language-learning disabled students* (pp. 65-104). San Diego: College-Hill.

Neuman, S.B., Copple, C. and Bredekamp, S. (2001). Phonological awareness in young children. *Scholastic Early Childhood Today, 15*(6), 11-15.

Norris, J.A. and Damico, J.S. (1990). Whole language in theory and practice: Implications for language intervention. *Language, Speech, and Hearing Services in Schools, 21*, 212-220.

Owens, R.E. (2004). *Language Disorders: A Functional Approach to Assessment and Intervention.* New York: Pearson Education, Inc.

Paulson, L.H., Kelly, K.L. Jepson, S., and van den Pol, R. (2004). The effects of an early reading curriculum on language and literacy development of

Head Start Children. *Journal of Research in Childhood Education, 18*(3), 169-179.

Roth, F.P., and Baden, B. (2001). Investing in Emergent Literacy Intervention: A Key Role for Speech-Language Pathologists. *Seminars in Speech and Language, 22*(3), 163-173.

Roth, F.P., Speece, F.L., and Cooper, D.H. (2002). A Longitudinal Analysis of the Connection between Oral Language and Early Reading. *The Journal of Educational Research, 95*(5), 295-272.

Share, D.L., and Leikin, M. (2004). Language impairment at school entry and later reading disability: Connections at lexical and supralexical levels of reading. *Scientific Studies of Reading, 8*(1), 87-110.

Shaughnessy, A. and Sanger, D (2005). Kindergarten Teachers' Perceptions of Language and Literacy Development, Speech Language Pathologists, and Language Interventions. *Communication Disorders Quarterly, 26*(2), 67-84.

Schuele, M. (2004). The Impact of Developmental Speech and Language Impairments on the Acquisition of Literacy Skills. *Mental Retardation and Developmental Disabilities Research Reviews, 10*, 176-183.

Snow, C.E., Scarborough, H.S. and Burns, M.S. (1999). What speech-language pathologists need to know about early reading. *Topics in Language Disorders, 20*(1), 48-59.

So, L.K.H., and Lam, C.S.L. (2000, July). Changing the roles of teachers and speech therapists. *International Special Education Conference.* Retrieved August 1, 2007, from http://www.isec2000.org.uk.htm

Tager-Flusberg, H. (1993). Putting words together: Morphology and syntax in the preschool years. In J.B. Gleason (Ed.), *The Development of Language* (3rd ed.) (pp. 195-237).

Wesseling, R. and Reitsma, P. (2001). Preschool phonological representations and development of reading skills. *Annals of Dyslexia, 51*, 203-230.

Westby, C.E. (1985). Learning to talk – Talking to learn: Oral-literate language differences. In C. Simon (Ed.), *Communication skills and classroom success: Therapy methodologies for language-learning disabled students.* San Diego: College-Hill.

In: Child and School Psychology
Editors: M. Haines et al., pp. 85-105
ISBN: 978-1-61470-801-8


*Chapter 3*

# MENTAL HEALTH PROVIDERS AND CHILDREN WITH MEDICAL CONDITIONS IN SCHOOLS

***L. Nabors[1]*, P. N. Ritchey[2], K. Sebera[1] and R. L. Ludke[3]***

[1]Counseling Program, School of Human Services, College of Education, Criminal Justice, and Human Services, University of Cincinnati, US
[2]Department of Sociology, College of Arts and Sciences, University of Cincinnati, US
[3]Department of Family and Community Medicine and Department of Public Health Sciences, University of Cincinnati Academic Health Center, US

## ABSTRACT

This chapter reviews the roles for mental health professionals working with children who have chronic medical conditions in schools. Mental health professionals have several roles in assisting children with chronic illnesses. For example, they are able network with teachers and school nurses to develop care plans to ensure that teachers understand and meet the special needs of children with medical conditions. Developing

---

* Correspondence: Dr. Nabors': telephone 513-556-5537 and email is naborsla@ucmail.uc.edu

written, individualized care plans is a way to ensure that the school and parents have a mutual understanding and acceptance of the best methods for meeting the child's needs to promote academic as well as social and emotional development. A section on health literacy reviews the importance of providing medical information in ways that teachers and children understand. Suggestions for working with children are provided from a noncategorical perspective, in that these ideas are helpful irrespective of the type of illness that the child is facing. Also, we present ideas for helping children who have cancer and cerebral palsy, as our examples of two specific illnesses. Ideas for future research are presented at the close of this chapter. Participatory research and single case designs are practical research designs for use in the schools, and these methods will allow professionals to focus on needs of the child within an ecological perspective.

Medical advances, often fueled by technological change, have improved lifestyles of children with medical conditions (University of Michigan Health System, 2005). These advances have resulted in increased inclusion of children with medical conditions in schools. Some of these children need support in school to cope with a range of issues, including social and emotional concerns as well as missed assignments and special learning needs. Approximately 40% of children with medical conditions experience difficulties at school, including absences and delays in academic progress (Thies and McAllister, 2001). Treatment plans and case management in schools facilitate inclusion and improve the school experiences of these children (Drotar, 2001). Mental health clinicians in schools are in a position to provide guidance by assisting with a myriad of issues faced by these children, such as coping with the side effects of medications, adherence to medical regimens and mental health problems (Nabors and Lehmkuhl, 2004).

## Medical Conditions: Definition and Prevalence

Our definition of chronic illness was developed by Stein and her colleagues (Stein, Westbrook, and Bauman, 1997). They defined a chronic illness as lasting for more than a year and as a condition resulting in limitations in social, physical, or mental health functioning compared to healthy peers. These researchers added that children with chronic medical conditions may need help with "…medications, special diet, medical technology, assistive devices, and personal assistance (p. 345)." Approximately 15% to 20% of the children in the United States have a chronic medical condition (Mescon and Honig, 1995). Most of the children with chronic illnesses, which we equate with chronic medical conditions, have moderate to mild levels of impairment, which means that they can participate in regular education settings, albeit with some special planning (Newacheck and Taylor, 1992; Thies and McAllister, 2001).

## Care Plans for Children with Medical Conditions

We recommend that children with chronic illnesses receive written care plans reviewed by their medical team. An example of a written care plan is presented in Table 1. The care plan should promote medical management and the child's development in the following areas: (1) physical functioning, (2) cognitive/academic functioning, and (3) social and emotional functioning. These areas are presented in the first column of Table 1. The role or function of key stakeholders should also be outlined in the plan. We have conceptualized these key stakeholders as being the child with an illness, parents, teachers, school nurses, the child's medical team, and the school mental health professional (see the first row of Table 1). Roles for stakeholders and the details of the plan should be listed for each area, by stakeholder. It is important to involve stakeholders to optimize the care plan. It can be a lot of work, but inviting all players to participate in developing the plan is an initial step. Research has shown that communication between the medical team and school may be a challenge (Nolan, Orlando, and Liptak, 2007). Thus, including the medical team in meetings is an important goal. A "case manager" or manager for the care plan should be selected and emergency contacts should be listed on the plan. Care plans should be updated; the interval for updating the plan should be established when the plan is created.

In terms of assistance, the mental health provider can provide input on physical management, including medication management and delivery, and ideas for ensuring that emergency care runs smoothly (see the final column in Table 1). The mental health provider can play a critical role in assessment of the child's cognitive and achievement skills.

## Table 1. Care Plan: Charting Roles of Stakeholders in School Planning Efforts

| Informant /Area | Child | Parent | Teacher | School Nurse | Medical Team | Mental Health |
|---|---|---|---|---|---|---|
| Physical<br>Change Environment | Extra books | Extra books; elevator | Extra time to get to classes | Provide Information | Provide Information | Provide information |
| Medication | Express needs | Make sure medications are at school | Respond to child requests | Have Meds available; back-up plan for administration | Provide plan; contact nurse for Med changes | Monitor Progress |
| Emergency Care | | | Understand care; know contacts | Medicines, first aid, know contacts | Work with school to develop plan | Provide information |
| Medical Regimen | Express needs<br><br>Diet, exercise | Share information with school team | Support adherence efforts | Provide input and assist in development of school plan | Work with school to develop plan | Coaching child, parent, teacher |
| Cognitive/ Academic | Complete homework ; attend tutoring | Check for missed assignments; contact teacher; tutor | Develop educational goals; provide make-up work | Provide Information | Provide information | Assessment of cognitive and academic functioning |
| Social and Emotional | Express needs; connect with peers | Provide information; ensure social opportunities are available | Support positive contacts with peers | Explain medical condition to peers | Provide information | Work with peers and child |
| Case Manager: | | Case Plan will be updated: | | Emergency contact numbers: | | |

These assessments are critical in developing educational planning and monitoring the child's progress. In terms of social and emotional functioning, the mental health professional can monitor the child's social environment (i.e., peer acceptance and social development) and provide individual counseling when necessary. Educating the child's classmates about his or her medical condition and how it influences the child's academic functioning and social interactions is another potential role for the mental health professional. Serving as a liaison, communicating about the child's needs and his or her development to other team members, is a role that is critical, although it is not listed in Table 1.

While the focus of this chapter is not on assessment, a thorough assessment of child's physical, cognitive, and social-emotional functioning is recommended; it should include meetings or contacts with the child's medical team to develop the care plan (Barrett, 2000). Another important source of information is the child's parents and potentially other family members, as a child's illness influences those who mobilize to support the child (Rolland, 1987; Shapiro, 2002). The school nurse or school district nurse is another key player to include in the development and implementation of care plans. The school nurse can serve as a "point person" in developing care plans in consultation with members of the medical team. The school nurse is a potential case manager as is the mental health professional at the child's school.

Medication management should be addressed under the "physical" section of the care plan. Children with chronic illnesses who take medications on an "as needed" basis have reported some difficulty in receiving medications at school (Smith, Taylor, Newbould, and Keady, 2008). Developing a system of medication access and administration for children with intermittent symptoms is important because symptoms wax and wane with many different illnesses. The American Academy of Pediatrics Committee on School Health (2003) has developed guidelines for administration of medications in schools, which is a useful resource.

We recommend that clinicians and school personnel use a "strengths-based focus" in order to maximize child success and integration within the classroom (Anderson, Loughlin, Goldberg, and Laffel, 2001). Care plans should be updated as needed, and at least yearly. We recommend that a "case manager" be appointed to ensure that the care plan is followed and updated. The case manager's role should include supporting the child by linking information between the medical and school settings and promoting communication among health care providers, schools, and families (Sexson and Madan-Swain, 1995). The person in this role needs to have dedicated or protected time to collaborate with the child, his or her parents, and the child's medical team. The school nurse is often first thought about as a case manager, but the school mental health professional or a teacher could perform this role.

If a care plan does not suffice, a next step is to develop a special education plan. A care plan can form the foundation for an Individual Education Plan (IEP) under the Section 504 label of "other health impaired" where comprehensive support, including the special education team at the school, is needed. The American Diabetes Association has developed a good example of a 504 plan (American Diabetes Association, 2004). This plan focuses on childhood diabetes, but it can be modified and serve as a template for a section 504 plan for other types of childhood chronic illnesses. Collaboration among parents, educators, and the medical team is important regardless of the plan type used to promote the child's wellness. Additionally, if parents or professionals need further information about the basic rights of persons with chronic medical conditions we recommend a book by Jaff (2010) entitled, "Know Your Rights: A Handbook for Patients with a Chronic Illness."

## CONSULTATION WITH TEACHERS

Many teachers have not had training in the area of childhood medical conditions and how these conditions influence child functioning. When beginning to work with teachers, an assessment of their knowledge of various chronic medical conditions as well as their confidence about working with children with various conditions provides a starting point for developing workshops or resources to enhance their knowledge (Johnson, Lubker, and Fowler, 1988; Nabors, Little, Akin-Little, and Iobst, 2008). Teachers also benefit from education about their role in working with children who have different types of illnesses. In most cases, teachers have a role as advisors for the child's cognitive/academic goals and provide input and assistance for adherence to the child's medical regimen at school (see Table 1). As mentioned, mental health professionals can support teachers with development of monitoring schedules and plans to boost adherence, assessment of cognitive functioning, and education of other children in the classroom to help them interact in a more positive way with the child.

Mental health professionals should inform teachers of their availability to provide ideas for supporting the child's social and emotional development (Clay, Cortina, Harper, Cocco, and Drotar, 2004). Mental health professionals can assist teachers by providing them with educational resources; a list of some potential resources is presented in Table 2.

**Table 2. Resources for Teachers and School Professionals Working with Children Who Have Chronic Illnesses**

| Resource | Description |
|---|---|
| Anderson and Dineen (2000). *Taking Cerebral Palsy to School.* | his book suggests interventions to improve the school experience of children with cerebral palsy. |
| Best et al. (2005). *Teaching Individuals with Physical or Multiple Disabilities: Fifth Edition.* | This text reviews ideas for curriculum adaptation and instructional strategies. Techniques for working with children with physical, neurological, and health problems are reviewed. |
| Closs (Editor, 2000). *The Education of Children with Medical Conditions.* | Chapters in this text review ideas for academic planning and promoting positive behavior in the classroom, and discuss psychosocial issues for children with chronic illness and their families. |
| McGrath and Johns (2008). *Reaching Students with Diverse Disabilities: Cross-Categorical Ideas and Activities.* | This book provides suggestions for improving children's social and emotional development as well as their language and math skills. The role of specialists and tips for completion of Individual Education plans are explained. |
| Nielsen, L. B. (2009). *Brief Reference of Student Disabilities… With Strategies for the Classroom: Second Edition.* | This book reviews information about regulations and laws, ideas for creating a positive learning environment, and strategies for educators for several different types of medical conditions. |
| Phelps (2006). *Chronic health-related disorders in children: Collaborative medical and psychoeducational interventions.* | This book presents ideas for assessment of children's needs for academic accommodations to enrich their learning and inclusion in the classroom for children with different types of medical conditions. |

Research shows that teacher education about the child's illness, what to do in an emergency, and how to enhance child inclusion and academic performance is an important component of services for children with chronic illness in schools (Clay et al., 2004; King, Tang, Ferguson, and DeBaun, 2005). The resources presented in Table 2 may be useful for parents, school administrators, and medical teams.

## IMPROVING HEALTH LITERACY OF CHILDREN, PARENTS, AND TEACHERS

Children, like adults, with chronic illnesses have complex medical management needs, and are likely taking multiple prescription and over-the-counter drugs. Thus, in a manner analogous to the chronic care model specified by Wagner (1998), a comprehensive approach to addressing the chronic medical conditions of children in school requires productive interactions between a prepared, proactive practice team and an informed activated child-parent dyad. Within the school context, the practice team includes not only the child's medical team, but also the teachers, staff, and health and mental health professionals within the schools who may need to be involved in the daily supervision or crisis management of the child's condition during school time.

Being an informed activated child-parent dyad requires that both the parents (or child's adult caregivers) and child be health literate, i.e., have the ability to obtain, process, and understand the basic health information and services they need to make appropriate health decisions, and be able to effectively communicate with each other in making informed and mutually agreeable decisions. However, research conducted to date has found that low literacy among adult caregivers of children is common and is associated with poor preventive care behaviors and poor child health outcomes (Sanders, Frederico, Klass, Abrams, and Dreyer, 2009). Caregivers of young children and adolescents with limited literacy skills have difficultly navigating complex health systems, understanding medical instructions and recommendations, performing child and self-care tasks, and understanding issues related to consent, medical authorization, and risk communication (Rothman et al., 2009). Chronically ill children who have adult caregivers with low literacy use more health services (Sanders et al. 2009) and have poorer control of their chronic illness (DeWalt et al., 2007). Of particular concern from a child safety perspective is the difficulties adult caregivers with low health literacy have in understanding prescription and over-the-counter drug labels, accurately interpreting medication dosing tables, and understanding medication administration instructions (Rothman et al., 2009). The very limited research on child literacy suggests that at least one out of every three adolescents and young adults have low health literacy and adolescents with low literacy are at least twice as likely to exhibit aggressive or antisocial behavior (Sanders et al. 2009). School mental health professionals who are involved in the treatment of a child with a chronic illness are in an ideal positive to design educational interventions through collaboration with the school nurse and the child's medical team. These interventions can become a cornerstone of counseling efforts because a lack of knowledge can be related to emotional and behavioral problems. School mental health professionals also can play a key role in providing information about the link between literacy and psychosocial problems when consulting with children's teachers.

But as noted by the Institute of Medicine, health literacy goes beyond the individual (Institute of Medicine, 2004) or even the child-parent dyad. It also depends upon the skills, preferences, and expectations of those providing the information, such as the doctors, nurses, administrators, home health workers, the media, and many others, which in the case of school includes teachers, mental health professionals, administrators, nurses, and other personnel. While research on the role of the health literacy of teachers and other school personnel on child health, particularly those children with chronic health conditions, is lacking, evidence clearly indicates that health materials distributed to parents and children are complex and often far exceed the average adult reading ability and that health professionals have limited skills, as well as patience, to work with persons of limited health literacy (Institute of Medicine, 2004). As such, the traditional paradigm of knowledge transfer from health information provider to the child-parent dyad must shift to one of building the self-efficacy of the dyad, motivating health-promoting behaviors, and evolving toward a paradigm of partnerships between the dyad and the health care team for decision-making, goal-setting, and self-management (Abrams, Klass, and Dreyer, 2009). As a team member, the school mental health professional can serve as an educator and also play a role in transmitting important health information between the child, parents, teacher, school nurse, and the child's medical team.

Any efforts to address health literacy of children and their parents/ caregivers must acknowledge the unique challenges of dealing with children as highlighted by Forrest, Simpson, and Clancy (1997) in their "4D" model. First, the developmental ability of the child, including his/her cognitive, emotional, and physical development must be given consideration. Maturational cognitive abilities may affect a child's health literacy abilities to understand and implement self-care as well as interact informatively with teachers and school-based health providers (Paiget, 1952). Second, there must be an understanding of the dependency between the child and his/her parents or other adult caregivers, particularly in regard to the transfer of self-care from the parents to the child. There are a number of factors which influence the transfer of medical care activities from parent to child and it is important to understand the relative responsibility of the parent and child for the child's ongoing care (DeWalt and Hink, 2009). Third, there must be an awareness of the differential epidemiology of health and illness in children compared to adults. This includes recognition of how the timing of a chronic illness may affect the cognitive development and health literacy skills as well as the psychosocial impact of the disease. Fourth, the child's demographics must be taken into account because of the relationship between socioeconomic disparities and health literacy; thus, the need to develop culturally and linguistically sensitive approaches to enhancing the health literacy of the child and family is important (DeWalt and Hink, 2009).

The next two sections of this chapter focus on two examples of illnesses, cancer and cerebral palsy. These were selected because children with either illness face unique challenges. The section on children with cancer, presents information on school re-entry or re-integration and peer acceptance, which are two areas of concern for children with many types of health problems. The section on children with cerebral palsy focuses on assessment of the child's skills and enriching positive relationships with peers as well as boosting self-esteem.

## Children with Cancer

Children who have cancer are at risk of social isolation and for falling behind in their school performance as they battle their disease and cognitive deficits related to cancer and its treatment (Nassau and Drotar, 1997). Often children with cancer need support for their academic performance. Rynard and colleagues provided excellent suggestions outlining roles for developing school support programs for children with cancer (Rynard, Chambers, Klinck, and Gray, 1998). Although this program is about helping youth with cancer, most of their recommendations addressed non-categorical or general issues faced by children with many types of chronic medical conditions. They described several key roles for mental health professionals in schools, including: (1) helping children cope with frequent absences; (2) providing counseling and support for parents and children; (3) teaching children strategies for coping with medical fears, (4) assisting children and families who must manage side-effects related to medical care; (5) developing interventions for the classroom as well as emergency medical plans; (6) consulting and collaborating with parents, school staff, and the medical team; (7) assisting in developing educational plans and developing plans to improve adherence to medication regimes, self-care at school, or classroom behaviors; (8) implementing assessments and interventions to improve academic and cognitive functioning; and (9) providing counseling and guidance for children to provide strategies and guidance to augment their abilities to cope with emotional and behavioral problems related to living with their illness.

Children with cancer may experience social isolation (Vance and Eiser, 2002). Mental health professionals working in schools may assist children in improving their relationships with their classmates and other friends attending their school. For instance, they can work with children in the classroom to help them understand the child's medical condition and special needs related to this condition. They can also work with the child with the condition, to improve his or her social skills or find him or her a "buddy" to assist with joining in group interactions (Sexon and Madan-Swain, 1995). Another idea would be to work on environmental change to improve the physical layout of recreational spaces, such as playgrounds, so that the child can more easily join in play and ongoing interactions (Nabors, McGrady, Rosenzweig, and Srivorakiat, 2007). Improving the child's relationships or assisting with the development of positive relationships with peers may be a resilience factor for children with cancer (Kim and Yoo, 2009).

Another area in which these children may need help is re-entering school after periods of illness-related absences (Vance, and Eiser, 2002). There is literature in this area to guide the development of programs and interventions for children with cancer who are returning to school and Table 3 presents a review of studies of school re-entry programs. Prevatt, Heffer, and Lowe (2000) provide a detailed review of school re-entry programs. Shaw and McCabe (2008) developed a reference that provides guidance for school re-entry. They review ideas for hospital-to-school transition for children with chronic illnesses, in light of new changes in the health care system. Children returning to school often benefit from tutoring, attending school for shortened periods of time, or having a temporary classroom aide to assist them in learning academic concepts they may not have learned prior to their hospitalization or extended absence from school.

**Table 3. Resources for School Re-Entry for Children with Cancer and Other Chronic Medical Conditions**

| Author | Description of School-Based Program |
|---|---|
| Van Eys (Ed.) (1982) | This book focuses on reintegration or inclusion of children with cancer in school settings. This book reviews psychosocial issues faced by the child and offers a window on parent and teacher perspectives. |
| Farmer and Peterson (1995) | This book covers assessments conducted to determine the child's academic needs, which are documented in an IEP. Sharing information with teachers is a key component of this program. |
| Worchell-Prevatt et al., (1998) | This book covers assessment of the child's academic and psychosocial needs. School-linked services consist of teacher education and classroom presentations to peers. |
| Barrett (2000) | This book describes how case managers serve as liaisons between the family, school and health care professionals, attend educational planning meetings, help coordinate health care appointments and missed homework, and provide educational information for school health care staff and teachers. |

Additionally, having a case manager, who interacts with the child's teacher and members of the medical team, may provide critical information for educators and school nurses. For example, a case manager can relay information from the medical team that improves the school environment for the child, such as allowing the child to take an elevator rather than the stairs when he or she has to switch floors to attend different classes (Sachs, 1980). A case manager also can assist in tutoring a child, finding a tutor and initiating the development of an individual education plan, and plan to assist the child in "catching up" on academic material he or she may have missed.

## CHILDREN WITH CEREBRAL PALSY

One of the difficulties in working with children diagnosed with cerebral palsy (CP) is that CP is an umbrella term covering a group of "non-progressive, but often changing, motor impairment syndromes," (Mutch et al., 1992, p. 547) which influence multiple areas of functioning in different ways in each child. Thus, a thorough assessment of the child's motor, cognitive, and social-emotional skills is needed to inform the development of care plans or other educational planning for children with CP.

Working with parents to understand the nature of the child's motor skills and personal strengths may be the best way to obtain an accurate picture of the child's skills (Kennes et al., 2002). Consultation with the child's doctor or member of his or her medical team will provide more data to inform school planning. In addition, we recommend using an assessment tool that captures the child's ability to perform daily activities, involving motor capabilities and intellectual functioning (Smits et al., 2011). For example, children with CP may not have the motor skills to explore and interact with their environments, which may negatively impact their incidental learning and interaction with others.

Assessment of the child's intellectual and achievement abilities will provide guidance for teachers. Teachers also need assistance and support in understanding how to help the child succeed in the classroom. When the teacher believes that the student can achieve, the student actually has not only improved self-confidence but also increased academic performance (Zimmerman, 1990).

Including evaluations from augmentative communication teams to determine ways for a child to provide and receive knowledge will inform school care plans. Furthermore, it may be beneficial to add questions or gather information about critical daily tasks involving motor skills at school, such as getting to the lunchroom or using the playground, being seated with peers during lunch, and special needs for riding buses and taking field trips.

Assessment of the child's social skills and emotional functioning and methods of coping with stress will allow the establishment of a baseline of the child's skills in these areas (Kennes et al., 2002; Freeborn and Mandleco, 2010). Then, the team working on the child's care plan can build upon these skills to facilitate positive relations with teachers and peers.

We suggest that teachers read and consider incorporating the book *Taking Cerebral Palsy to School* (Anderson and Dineen, 2000) in their classroom to facilitate better understanding of CP and the experiences of children with this diagnosis. Improving peers' knowledge of the child's skills and limitations also needs to be addressed in care plans, because like children with cancer (Vance and Eiser, 2002), children with CP are at risk of facing rejection by peers and experiencing feelings of isolation at school (Nadeau and Tessier, 2009). Rather than focusing on limitations, the team can use a strengths-based perspective to find common interests and activities for children with CP to interact meaningfully with their peers. Teachers can use or adapt activities and cooperative projects to allow for further integration in the classroom. Physical and occupational therapists, along with physical education teachers, can work to find ways to incorporate children with physical disabilities into recreational play during recess and gym class that can be both therapeutic and provide needed social interaction.

Children with CP may have difficulty building a positive self-concept as they experience feeling different from their peers and may often be labeled as "handicapped." Mental health professionals can work with these children in developing a healthy self-concept and coping with any negative feelings about how cerebral palsy affects their daily living. Assessment of child coping skills – both positive and negative – will provide a picture of the child's resources and his or her abilities to be resilient when experiencing difficulties (Freeborn and Mandleco, 2010). This information can be a cornerstone of interventions. Working with the child, teacher, and the child's classmates to improve acceptance and the positive nature of interactions could vastly improve the child's experiences in the school setting.

The final sections of this chapter review ideas for future research. These sections serve to provide ideas for research in the field. In our concluding paragraph, we offer a summary of critical issues for children with medical conditions in schools and highlight the importance of care plans and a team approach for optimizing medical management in schools.

## Ideas for Future Research in Schools

Our review of the literature generated several ideas for future research. Research to establish the level of teachers' health literacy and determine the assistance they require to help a child with a chronic illness in the classroom is needed. Studying the effectiveness of care plans will provide information about whether written plans are a helpful educational tool. Another important area for research is the functioning of siblings of children with chronic illnesses. Although this was not a focus of this chapter, these children may feel isolated and experience problems in school (Alderfer and Hodges, 2010). Thus, evaluation of siblings' needs for school support could be a role for school mental health professionals when working with children and families.

Another area for consideration is research on the process of medication management in the schools (Smith et al., 2008). For example, more information is needed about barriers to medication administration and adherence to the regimen for taking medication in schools. We also know little about the social impact of medication management in schools in terms of whether administration of medicine in the classroom, such as insulin by children with diabetes, influences peers' attitudes toward children who have chronic medical conditions. Information is also lacking about the impact of nonmedical staff administering medications at school.

Children in rural areas may experience problems accessing medical care. Telehealth is a growing field and electronic communications can be one way to connect children in remote areas to care. This method also may be optimal for transfer of medical information from the child's own medical team to the school nurse and other members of the child's school-based team. Research has shown that school personnel may not always be comfortable with using telecommunications to discuss a child's care (Spaulding, Davis, and Patterson, 2008). Holding an "in-person" meeting prior to teleconferencing might be a way to initiate the development of personal relationships, increasing the likelihood that participants are more comfortable with electronic methods of communication in large group formats. Also, discussing an outline for the meeting prior to beginning a team meeting may improve the flow of these "electronic meetings." Further research on the use of telemedicine and telehealth conferences in rural schools will provide information to evaluate the effectiveness of this method for developing care plans.

Another idea for research is conducting single subject design or case studies to document the process of school-based care and the successes and failures in this process for children with different types of chronic illnesses. Documenting what does and does *not* work for children with different types of illness can provide a "window" on specific experiences for children with different illnesses. Moreover, recording steps in the process of care can serve as a blueprint for other parents as they and their child work with school personnel to develop plans for medical management at school. We recommend that these studies include qualitative and quantitative methods to record success stories, which will offer support and guidance for other parents whose children have the same medical diagnosis. Participatory approaches to research that showcase the "voice" of children and parents and key stakeholders in schools, will help to document unfolding stories and will contribute to knowledge about the process of medical management in schools. Some of the critical issues to document include: (1) barriers to peer relationships or experiences of isolation (Vance and Eiser, 2002), (2) school re-entry (Shaw and McCabe, 2008), (3) methods to improve health literacy of children, parents and teachers (DeWalt and Hink, 2009), (4) aspects of positive relationships with teachers and peers (Freeborn and Mandleco, 2010; Kim and Yoo, 2009), and (5) the development and implementation of classroom interventions (Rynard et al., 1998).

School mental health professionals may serve as evaluators and assess the aforementioned research topics. Alternately, they can be part of an evaluation team assessing these topics. Evaluators also can play a role by assessing progress in child health and academic functioning for children with medical conditions attending a particular school or school district. School mental health professionals also need to examine the effectiveness of the services they provide. For example, understanding the "most optimal therapy dose" for children with medical conditions who also exhibit internalizing or externalizing behavior problems is a potential area for treatment-focused research. The effectiveness of individual therapy versus bringing a friend to sessions to act as a support person is another possible area for research.

# Conclusions

In her editorial, Wilma Peebles-Wilkins (2006) summarized critical points for school professionals to consider when working with a child who has a medical condition:

> "Help recognize the signs of the illness and how it affects the specific child. Know how to respond if the child has an episode at school. Help with cognitive functioning and building confidence. Be calm and accepting. Create a favorable social climate in the school environment" (p. 67).

Following these guidelines as "rules of thumb" for including children with medical conditions in the classroom can help these children to thrive in the school setting. Moreover, developing specialized care plans is helpful on two levels. First, these plans inform teachers and staff about each child's needs so that they can respond appropriately. Second, it is important to provide education to school staff so that they have an opportunity to understand a child's special needs and critical issues for the child's medical care. The school mental health professional plays a role in developing the plans, assessing child cognitive, social, and emotional functioning, and evaluating child participation and adjustment in the school setting. Providing counseling as well as measuring the impact of interventions on child academic progress or social functioning are other potential roles. The school mental health professional may serve as a case manager, guiding the development of and ensuring the implementation of the child's care plan. As a case manager or care plan manager it will be important to emphasize a team approach, involving the child, parent, medical team and other school staff in developing and implementing the care plan. We advocate the development of care plans with yearly meetings to update the plans as a means to support the child as he or she navigates through difficulties and begins to thrive at school.

## REFERENCES

Abrams, M. A., Klass, P., and Dreyer, B. P. (2009). Health literacy and children: recommendations for action. *Pediatrics, 124*, S327-331.

Alderfer, M. A., and Hodges, J. A. (2010). Supporting siblings of children with cancer: A need for family-school partnerships. *School Mental Health, 2*(2), 72-81.

American Academy of Pediatrics, Committee on School Health (2003). Guidelines for the administration of medication at school. *Pediatrics, 112*(3), 697-699.

American Diabetes Association (2004). Co-Sponsor: Disability Rights Education and Defense Fund. *Sample Section 504 Plan*. Retrieved on February 21, 2011 from http://www.ibsgroup.org/chronickids/504.pdf.

Anderson, M.E. and Dineen, T. (2000). *Taking cerebral palsy to school.* Jayjo Books.

Anderson, B., Loughlin, C., Goldberg, E., and Laffel, L. (2001). Comprehensive, family-focused outpatient care for very young children living with chronic disease: Lessons learned from a program in pediatric diabetes. *Children's Services: Social Policy, Research, and Practice, 4*, 235-250.

Barrett, J. T. (2000). A school-based care management service for children with special needs. *Family and Community Health, 23,* 36-42.

Best, S. J., Wolff-Heller, K., and Bigge, J. L. (2005). *Teaching Individuals with Physical or Multiple Disabilities: Fifth Edition*. Upper Saddle River, NJ: Pearson: Merrill Prentice Hall.

Clay, D., Cortina, S., Harper, D., Cocco, K., and Drotar, D. (2004). Schoolteachers' experiences with childhood chronic illness. *Children's Health Care, 33*(3), 227-239.

Closs, A. (Ed.) (2000). *The education of children with medical conditions*. London: David Fulton Publishers.

DeWalt, D. A., Dilling, M. H., Rosenthal, M. S., and Pignone, M. P. (2007). Low parental literacy is associated with worse asthma care measures in children. *Ambulatory Pediatrics, 7*(1), 25-31.

DeWalt, D. A., Hink, A. (2009). Health literacy and child health outcomes: a systematic review of the literature. *Pediatrics, 124*, S265-S274.

Drotar, D. (2001). Promoting comprehensive care for children with chronic health conditions and their families: Introduction to the special issue. *Children's Services: Social Policy, Research, and Practice, 4*, 157-163.

Farmer, J. E., and Peterson, L. (1995). Pediatric traumatic brain injury: Promoting successful school reentry. *School Psychology Review, 24*, 230-243.

Forrest, C. B., Simpson, L., and Clancy, C. (1997). Child health services research: Challenges and opportunities. *Journal of the American Medical Association, 277*(22), 1787–1793.

Freeborn, D., and Mandleco, B. (2010). Childhood educational experiences of women with cerebral palsy. *Journal of School Nursing, 26*(4), 310-319.

Institute of Medicine. (2004). *Health Literacy: A Prescription to End Confusion*. Washington, DC: National Academies Press.

Jaff, J. C. (2010). *Know your rights: A handbook for patients with chronic illness*. Farmington, CT: Advocacy for Patients with Chronic Illness.

Kennes, J., Rosenbaum, P., Hanna, S. E., Walter, S., Russell, D., Parminder, R., Bartlett, D., and Galuppi, B. (2002). Health status of school-aged children with cerebral palsy: Information from a population-based sample. *Developmental Medicine and Child Neurology, 44*, 240-247.

Kim, D. H., and Yo, I. Y. (2009). Factors associated with resilience of school age children with cancer. *Journal of Paediatrics and Child Health, 46*, 431-436.

King, A.A., Tang, S., Ferguson, K.L., and DeBaun, M.R. (2005). An education program to increase teacher knowledge about sickle cell disease. *Journal of School Health, 75*(1), 11-14.

McGrath, M. Z., and Johns, B. H. (2008). *Reaching students with diverse disabilities: Cross categorical ideas and activities*. Lanham, MD: Rowman and Littlefield Education.

Mescon, J. A. W., and Honig, A. S. (1995). Parents, teachers and medical personnel: Helping children with chronic illness. *Early Child Development and Care, 111*, 107-129.

Mutch, L., Alberman, E., Hagberg, B., Kodama, K., and Velickovic, P.M. (1992). Cerebral palsy epidemiology: Where are we now and where are we going? *Developmental Medicine and Child Neurology, 34,* 547-551.

Nabors, L., and Lehmkuhl, H. (2004). Children with chronic medical conditions: Recommendations for school mental health clinicians. *Journal of Developmental and Physical Disabilities, 16*, 1-15.

Nabors, L. A., Little, Steven, G., Akin-Little, A., Iobst, E. A. (2008). Teacher knowledge and confidence in meeting the needs of children with chronic medical conditions: Pediatric psychology's contribution to education. *Psychology in the Schools, 45*(3), 217-226.

Nabors, L. A., McGrady, M. E., Rosenzweig, K. J., and Srivorakiat, L. (2007). Improving the competence of preschoolers with disabilities on playgrounds. *Early Childhood Services, 4*, 235-247.

Nadeau, L., and Tessier, R. (2009). Social adjustment at school: Are children with cerebral palsy perceived more negatively by their peers than other at-risk children? *Disability and Rehabilitation, 31*(4), 302-308.

Nassau, J. H., and Drotar, D. (1997). Social competence among children with central nervous system-related chronic health conditions: A review. *Journal of Pediatric Psychology, 22*, 771-793.

Newacheck, P. W., and Taylor, W. R. (1992). Chronic childhood illness: Prevalence, severity, and impact. *American Journal of Public Health, 82*(3), 364-371.

Nielsen, L. B. (2009). *Brief reference of student disabilities...with strategies for the classroom*. Thousand Oaks, CA: Corwin Press: Sage.

Nolan, K. W., Orlando, M., and Liptak, G. S. (2007). Care coordination services for children with special health care needs: Are we family-centered yet? *Families, Systems, and Health, 25*(3), 293-306.

Peebles-Wilkins, W. (2006). Editorial: Responding to children with chronic illness. *Children and Schools, 28*, 67-68.

Phelps, L. (Ed.) (2006). *Chronic health-related disorders in children: Collaborative medical and psychoeducational interventions*. Washington DC: American Psychological Association.

Piaget, J. (1952). *The Origins of Intelligence in Children.* New York, NY: International Universities Press.

Prevatt, F. F., Heffer, R. W., and Lowe, P. A. (2000). A review of school reintegration programs for children with cancer. *Journal of School Psychology, 38*, 447-467.

Rolland, J. S. (1987). Chronic illness and the life cycle: A conceptual framework. *Family Process, 26*, 203-221.

Rothman, R. L., Yin, H. S., Mulvaney, S., Co, J.P.T., Homer, C., and Lannon, C. (2009). Health literacy and quality: Focus on chronic illness care and patient safety. *Pediatrics, 124* (Supplement 3), S315-S326.

Rynard, D. W., Chambers, A., Klinck, A. M., and Gray, J. D. (1998). School support programs for chronically ill children: Evaluating adjustment of children with cancer at school. *Children's Health Care, 27*, 31-46.

Sachs, M. B. (1980). Helping the child with cancer go back to school. *The Journal of School Health, 50,* 328-331.

Sanders, L. M., Federico, S., Klass, P., Abrams, M.A., and Dreyer, B. (2009). Literacy and child health: a systematic review. *Archives of Pediatric and Adolescent Medicine, 163*, 131-140.

Sexson, S., and Madan-Swain, A. (1995). The chronically ill child in school. *School Psychology Quarterly, 10*, 359-368.

Shaw, S., and McCabe, P. (2008). Hospital-to-school transition for children with chronic illness: Meeting the new challenges of an evolving health care system. *Psychology in the Schools, 45* (1), 74-87.

Shapiro, E. (2002). Chronic Illness as a family process: a social-developmental approach to promoting resilience. *Psychotherapy in Practice 58* (11), 1375-1384.

Smith, F. J., Taylor, K. M. G., Newbould, J., and Keady, S. (2008). Medicines for chronic illness at school: Experiences and concerns of young people and their parents. *Journal of Clinical Pharmacy and Therapeutics, 33*(5), 537-544.

Smits, D-W., Ketelaar, M., Willem Gorter, J., van Schie, P., Dallmeijer, A., Jongmans, M., and Lindeman, E. (2011). Development of daily activities in school-age children with cerebral palsy. *Research in Developmental Disabilities, 32*, 222-234.

Spaulding, R. J., Davis, K., and Patterson, J. (2008). A comparison of telehealth and face-to-face presentation for school professionals supporting students with chronic illnesses. *Journal of Telemedicine and Telecare, 14*(4), 211-214.

Stein, R. E. K., Westbrook, L. E., and Bauman, L. J. (1997). *The Questionnaire for Indentifying Children with Chronic Conditions*: A measure based on a noncategorical approach. *Pediatrics, 99*, 513-521.

Thies, K. M., and McAllister, J. M. (2001). The Health Education and Leadership Project: A school initiative for children and adolescents with chronic health conditions. *Journal of School Health, 71*, 167-172.

University of Michigan Health System. (2005). Your Child | Children with Chronic Conditions. Retrieved February 20, 2011 from, *http://www.med.umich.edu/1libr/yourchild/chronic.htm*.

Vance, Y. H., and Eiser, C. (2002). The school experience of the child with cancer. *Child: Care, Health, and Development, 28*, 5-19.

Van Eys, J. (Ed.) (1982). *Children with cancer: Mainstreaming and reintegration*. New York: SP Medical and Scientific Books.

Wagner, E. H. (1998). Chronic disease management: What will it take to improve care for chronic illness? *Effective Clinical Practice, 1*(1), 2-4.

Worchel-Prevatt, F. F., Heffer, R. W., Prevatt, B. C., Miner, J., Young-Saleme, T., Horgan, D., Lopez, M., Rae, W. A., and Frankel, L. (1998). A school reentry program for chronically ill children. *Journal of School Psychology, 36*, 261-279.

Zimmerman, B.J. (1990). Self-regulated learning and academic achievement: An overview. *Educational Psychologist, 25*(1), 3-17.

In: Child and School Psychology ISBN: 978-1-61470-801-8
Editors: M. Haines et al., pp. 107-123 

*Chapter 4*

# STRESS ED: THE ACADEMIC AND SOCIAL-EMOTIONAL BENEFITS OF INCLUDING MINDFULNESS-BASED STRESS REDUCTION (MBSR) IN K-12 EDUCATION

***Amy Saltzman[a] and David S. Black*[b]***

[a] The Still Quiet Place, Menlo Park, CA, US

[b] Institute for Health Promotion and Disease Prevention Research,
Keck School of Medicine,
University of Southern California, Los Angeles, CA, US

## ABSTRACT

Schools offer a variety of educational programs, such as Drivers' Ed and Sex Ed, to promote youth's responsible behavior, protect their health, and increase their ability to learn. Given the protective benefits of such educational efforts, and the pervasive stresses children and adolescents face on a daily basis, schools must also educate youth about how to cope effectively with psychological stress. Stress has a major influence on child and adolescent psychology, and contributes to depression, anxiety, eating disorders, addictions, suicide and other psychological and health

---

* Correspondence to: David S. Black. University of Southern California, 1000 S. Fremont Avenue, Unit #8, Building A-5, Alhambra, CA 91803-4737, E-mail: davidbla@usc.edu

ailments. Stress also has a negative impact on learning. Therefore, it is important that stress reduction be incorporated into school-based education to promote learning, pro-social behavior, and well-being.

This chapter discusses the concept of stress education (Stress Ed), a mindfulness based stress reduction curriculum, and how such a curriculum might minimize student distress, enhance learning, and increase pro-social behavior. We first describe the prevalence of child and adolescent stress-related disorders and the impact of these disorders on academic learning, healthy social development, and risk taking behaviors. Then, we describe the essential components of mindfulness-based stress reduction (MBSR) programs as a foundation for creating Stress Ed curricula. Next, we review the preliminary data regarding the benefits of offering MBSR and related mindfulness programs to K-12 students. Finally, we discuss the current challenges to school-based Stress Ed and offer potential solutions.

**Keywords:** Stress Ed, mindfulness-based stress reduction, school-based, education.

Schools offer a variety of educational programs to promote the responsible behavior of youth, protect their health and well-being, and increase their ability to learn. For example, drivers' education (Drivers' Ed) prevents accident-related disability and mortality, sexual education (Sex Ed) protects against sexually transmitted infection and unintended pregnancy, and drug and alcohol education (Drug Ed) prevents against substance misuse and abuse. These programs have proven merit in protecting the health of our nation's youth through awareness building, education, and subsequent behavioral change (e.g., Cuijpers, 2002; Elder et al., 2005; Kirby et al., 1994); however, educational programs for addressing the detrimental effects of stress are relatively underdeveloped.

Stress has a significant negative impact on the health and academic performance of children and adolescents, yet it is rarely addressed with formal preventive school-based programming to the extent of other educational programs mentioned previously. Because stress is present in elementary, middle, and high school, stress reduction is important in each one of these contexts. In fact, many of the poor choices and unhealthy behaviors that we aim to prevent with existing school-based programs are intricately related to stress and stress-related disorders such as anxiety and depression. Therefore, its is essential that schools provide formalized school-based programming with the aim of supporting students in developing the skills necessary for dealing responsively and effectively with psychological stress. For the purposes of this chapter we refer to such programming as stress education (Stress Ed).

## Student Stress

Psychological stress is pervasive among school-age youth in the United States. This stress has significant and detrimental effects not only on adolescent health, but also on learning. Students must balance multiple developmental tasks simultaneously: learning academic material, navigating peer and family relationships, participating in extracurricular activities, and perhaps most importantly "growing-up" in a fast-paced culture with pervasive social challenges and high demand for success. As a consequence, many students suffer from the stresses of striving to succeed: maintaining high academic standing, participating in competitive extracurricular activities, and seeking college admission. Still other students suffer from financial strain, illness and disability, interpersonal conflict, and abuse and violence in their homes and communities.

Students often report feeling overwhelmed by and unable to cope with the stressors they face in daily life; this finding has important implications for child and adolescent mental health. Conservatively, at least 5% (~3.2 million) of children in the United States ages 4-17 years old have emotional or behavioral difficulties, and for 80% of these children, these difficulties impact their family life, friendships, learning, leisure activities and general functioning (Simpson et al., 2005). Moreover, approximately 50% of children with these difficulties are actively upset or distressed by their emotional or behavioral difficulties. Such frustration compounds the pre-existing feelings of being stressed (Simpson et al., 2005). This accumulated stress is likely contributing to unprecedented and alarming rates of depression, anxiety, eating disorders, cutting, addictions, suicide, and other self-destructive behaviors documented in the United States and in other nations. For example, stress and its associated psychological disorders are associated with cruelty, bullying and violence among children and adolescents (Craig, 1998). Stress-influenced behavior, such as acting out and bullying, is disruptive to peers and the general learning environment, and contributes to the emotional and behavioral difficulties faced by youth (Leung and To, 2009).

Stress and its associated psychological disorders prevail across all socio-economic levels (Blum et al., 2000). Historically, it had been presumed that children of affluence were at lower risk for mental health ailments; however, research has documented that affluent suburban youth can score significantly higher on anxiety, depression, and frequency of cigarettes, alcohol, and other illicit drug use than less affluent youth (Luthar and D'Avanzo, 1999). Related studies have found that affluent youth are at an increased risk for psychological ailments, and are more likely to report using drugs than a nationally representative sample of youth from lower socio-economic backgrounds who attend school (Bogard, 2005). This has led reserchers to recommend that, in addtion to supporting youth from lower socio-economic settings, greater attention need be paid to addressing the psychological needs of affluent youth (Luthar, 2003).

Finally, stressors also compound the difficulties of children with special needs such as those with learning disabilities, and these youth are at even greater risk of suffering from depression, anxiety, and suicide than are their typical stressed peers (Bender, Rosenkrans and Crane, 1999; Geisthardt and Munsch, 1996; Maag and Reid, 2006). Children with learning disabilities also may be especially sensitive to challenges in school, as they report higher stress levels resulting from interacting with teachers and taking performance tests (Alexander-Passe, 2008). The stress encountered in youth can also have lasting effects.

## Lasting Effects of Stress

Stress during childhood and adolescence can have detrimental effects that last into adulthood. A study of over 17,000 adult respondents who reported their life histories of stressful events (Middlebrooks and Audage, 2008) documented the prevalence and effects of childhood stress across the lifespan. The report showed that adverse childhood stressors including abuse, neglect, and household dysfunction were very common among respondents from all socio-economic backgrounds; almost 67% of the sample reported at least one adverse childhood stressor. Moreover, this research showed that almost 13% of respondents reported 4 or more such stressful childhood events. It is well understood that facing multiple stressors in early years place youth at risk for health and behavioral problems in adulthood, including substance abuse, depression, suicide attempts, and violence.

The stresses encountered in childhood and adolescence can impede later healthy development in several ways. This is due, in part, to the fact that brain development is especially sensitive during childhood and adolescence, and that disruptions in these developmental processes predispose individuals to psychiatric disorders and other conditions (Weber et al., 2008). More specifically, traumatic stressors predispose youth to psychopathology such as anxiety and depression (Copeland et al., 2007) and can also lead to lasting impediments to normal brain development (Frodl et al., 2010). For example, prolonged exposure to stress can disrupt the connection of brain circuits. In extreme cases this disruption can result in decreased brain size and reduced threshold for stress, thereby making people overly reactive to adverse experiences throughout life. In addition, sustained and high levels of cortisol (a primary hormone released in response to a stressor) can damage the hippocampus, an area of the brain responsible for learning and memory (Majer et al., 2010; Middlebrooks and Audage, 2008; Pechtel and Pizzagalli, 2011).

Due to its influence on the structure and function of the brain, stress can also impede students' cognitive performance. For example, research has found that the chronic stress of childhood poverty is inversely related to working memory. Working memory is one of the processes of executive function, which is the control unit of advanced cognitive processing (Bos et al., 2009; Colvert et al., 2008) that promotes goal-directed behavior such as completing a tasks while minimizing distractions and is essential in language compreension, reading, problem solving, and memory (Evans and Schamberg, 2009). Interestingly, many children who experience early life stressors have impaired intellectual ability, worsened academic performance, and a greater need for individualized education programs (Pechtel and Pizzagalli, 2011). Moreover, disruption in brain networks from prolonged stress in childhood is associated with a reduction in reward pursuing behavior (Anisman and Matheson, 2005). Thus students with a history of prolonged stress may not be motivated by pro-social rewards such as positive feedback from teachers or graduating from high school. It is also important to note that some groups such as youth with learning disabilities, poor impulse control, and/or attention deficit hyperactivity disorder (ADHD) may be especially sensitive to the cognitive detriments resulting from stress.

In the previous section, we have highlighted some of the data regarding the detrimental effects of stress to the health and academic performance of youth. These findings suggest that schools should provide effective programming to help students cope effectively with stress and therefore prevent lasting psychological and academic problems. Next, we describe the fundamental elements of the mindfulness-based stress reduction (MBSR) program, and variations of the mindfulness-based Stress Ed curricula that may help youth develop techniques to cope with stress and thus prevent stress-related ailments and promote mental health.

## STRESS ED: FUNDAMENTALS OF THE MINDFULNESS-BASED STRESS REDUCTION (MBSR) PROGRAM

The mindfulness-based stress reduction (MBSR) program and related mindfulness programs have shown promise in helping youth cope with stress, and in reducing the impact of stress on their ability to learn. MBSR programs use a variety of techniques to support the cultivation of mindfulness as means of reducing stress. Over 30 years of research evaluating the effectiveness of mindfulness among adults has shown that mindfulness can decrease stress, depression, anxiety, and hostility, and enhances executive function, compassion and empathy (Chambers, Lo and Allen, 2008; Kabat-Zinn, 1982; Kabat-Zinn, Lipworth and Burney, 1985; Kabat-Zinn, Lipworth, Burncy and Sellers, 1986; Kabat-Zinn et al., 1992; Shapiro, Schwartz and Bonner, 1998). A smaller, yet growing, area of research has begun to indicate that children and adolescents can garner some of these same benefits.

A common definition of *mindfulness* used when working with school-aged children is: *paying attention to your life, here and now, with kindness and curiosity, and then choosing your behavior.* Youth, as well as adults, have the unique capacity to pay attention to and be aware of our internal and external worlds and the interactions between these worlds. We can attend to the breath, the five senses, thoughts, and emotions--the combined processes which create our impulses and actions--and how our behavior affects our well-being and the well-being of those we come in contact with. This ability to focus and maintan attention is a natural innate human capacity.

The practice of mindfulness teaches students how to orient their attention to the present moment with an attitude of non-judgmental acceptance. This specific way of paying attention has the potentional to enhance both academic and social-emotional learning. Over the last decade mindfulness practices have been introduced to thousands of students in diverse schools settings throughout the United States and internationally. Several well established mindfulness-based Stress Ed curricula (Still Quiet Place[1], Inner Kids[2], Stressed Teens [3], Wellness Works[4], Mindful Schools[5]) have been implemented in individual classrooms, entire schools, and throughout school districts, as well as in clinical settings.

---

[1] www.stillquietplace.com
[2] www.innerkids.org
[3] www.stressedteens.com
[4] www.wellnessworksinschools.com
[5] www.mindfulschools.org

Mindfulness-based Stress Ed programs include specific instruction on attending to the breath, the five senses, thoughts, and emotions. Only experienced staff with long-term personal mindfulness practices teach these courses. The effectiveness of such programs, like any school curricula -- math, drama, language arts, sports -- depends on the teacher's experience and understanding of the subject and their ability to connect with students. One sample curricula is the "Still Quiet Place course," created by Dr. Amy Saltzman. Based on that curriculum, we now describe a typical sequence of practices that can be used to teach mindfulness-based Stress Ed to school-age children.

In the initial stages of the curriculum, students learn to pay attention to the flow of the in-breath and the out-breath, noticing when the mind wanders, and returning the attention to the breath after the mind wanders. This practice is usually calming and it is intended to strengthen attention over time, and to help students develop the capacity for observing their present moment experience. Students then develop body awareness both by slowly sweeping attention through the body from toes to head while noting the sensations in each area, and by attending to a specific sense perceptions such as taste or sound. Again these practices intend to develop students' capacity for observing present moment experience, and help students become familiar with body-oriented cues to distressing thoughts and emotions such as the nervous energy of anxiety, the headache of frustration, or the jaw-tightening of anger.

Students are then invited to observe their thoughts. Over time they may realize that thoughts come and go just like the breath or physical sensations. Through this practice they learn that thoughts (particularly negative mental chatter) are common, temporary, and frequently untrue. Next, students are encouraged to bring their increasingly refined attention to their emotions, noticing emotions as they arise, noticing how their emotions manifest physically in the body, and noticing how thoughts, emotions, physical sensations are interconnected. The intention of this practice is to support students to "have their feelings, without their feelings having them." This means they are able to observe their feelings without automatically reacting to them. These foundational instructions are followed by practices that use the awareness of internal experience to support students in responding effectively rather than reacting ineffectively to difficult situations, and in cultivating attitudes of compassion and kindness toward themselves and others.

In most curricula, students also learn gentle stretching or yoga practices. These exercises teach students physical, mental and emotional balance, which requires a series of contuinous adjustments. These activities also give students an opportunity to investigate how they approach new and challenging activities. During our mindfulness-based activities, students often talk about their experiences with mindfulness. For example, one fourth-grade boy described his use of mindfulness as follows: "I was on the playground at recess. A kid said something mean to me. I wanted to hit him. But, I took a breath, and walked away." This was a breakthrough for this particular boy, who frequently had altercations on the playground that ended with him being sent to the principal's office. Mindfulness allowed him to notice the thought "I want to hit him," breathe, and then to choose a new and constructive response.

In summary, mindfulness develops the natural capacities of awareness, attention, and choice, which are capacities that can help everyone, and especially those students who struggle in academic and other social contexts. A student can become aware of the negative internal chatter such as, "I can't do this math problem," "I am dumb," "I am going to fail," "Maybe I'll just drop out," and then choose to take a few deep breaths, refocus attention on the math problem at hand, and respond to the situation it in new and novel ways.

## FORMAT FOR STRESS ED CURRICULA

Most established Mindfulness Based Stress Ed curricula offer practices similar to those described above, and can be tailored to youth of all ages and learning needs. The basic format for students in grades K-2 tends to be common across curricula. Sessions typically last 15-30 minutes, and usually include 1-2 brief practices interspersed with short discussions, mindful movement activities, and/or mindful games.

For older students, the curricular formats vary more widely. Still Quiet Place, Inner Kids, Stressed Teens and Wellness Works employ trained mindfulness instructors to offer 30-60 minute weekly, or bi-weekly classes in schools, afterschool programs, community and clinical settings, for at least 8 weeks. Mindful Schools has trained mindfulness instructors to offer 15-minute sessions to every class in a given school, 3 times per week for 5 weeks. Trained school counselors can implement either the 8-week or 5-week formats with sessions led by the counselor, either in the regular classroom or by referall to a group pull-out session.

Each format has benefits and limitations. The longer weekly sessions allow for more in-depth exploration of the application of mindfulness to the daily stresses students face inside and outside the classroom. Students may become distracted or disruptive during longer discussions, but such issues provide teachable moments whereby students can investigate disruptive and disrespectful habits and impulses to be "cool" or cruel, as they arise. This can be helpful, since the same thoughts and feelings that lead students to act out during mindfulness class lead to similar behavior in other settings such as the classroom and cafeteria. The briefer and more frequent sessions provide consistency over time, but do not allow the students as much time to explore the use of mindfulness in daily life.

In a third format, an individual counselor or classroom teacher with an established mindfulness practice incorporates the training into his/her standard daily routine. This format allows for consistency over time, and can be especially useful to help students deal with the stresses of class work, homework, and test-taking. Although only a limited number of counselors and teachers currently have the requisite mindfulness training, this limitation is changing rapidly.

Mindfulness programs have been offered in almost every type of school setting: public schools, affluent independent schools, and underserved schools. Mindfulness training has been offered in individual classrooms, in small "pull-out, referral" groups, where teacher or staff referred students are pulled from their regularly scheduled coursework, in alternative learning, special education, detention, and probation programs, as well as school-based programs for pregnant teens and teen mothers, athletes, and performing artists. Any counselor or teacher with adequate training in mindfulness can adapt and combine the components of various curricula to tailor sessions to the scheduling constraints, issues, intended outcomes, and reflective abilities of a particular group of students. Interestingly, many colleges and some high schools are incorporating mindfulness into a wide variety of curricula from Architecture to Theater Arts[6]

## EVIDENCE FOR MINDFULNESS-BASED PROGRAMS AMONG YOUTH

The majority of evidence regarding the efficacy of MBSR and related mindfulness programs comes from research studies conducted among adults (for a comprehensive database on mindfulness research, see[7]). However, a handful of studies reveal promising evidence about the effectiveness of

[6] http://www.acmhe.org/index.php?option=com_content&view=article&id=23&Itemid=82

[7] http://www.mindfulexperience.org

mindfulness-based Stress Ed programs for K-12 students. For example, a randomized controlled trial (RCT) demonstrated first, second, and third graders who participated in a bi-weekly, 12-session integrative program of mindfulness and relaxation had significant increases in attention and social skills, and decreases in test anxiety and ADHD behaviors (Napoli, 2004). A second RCT compared a mindfulness based program, practiced for 30 minutes twice a week for 8 weeks, to a quiet reading condition among an ethnically diverse children ages 7-9 in an elementary school setting (Flook et al., 2010). In this study, teacher and parent reports showed that children with poorer initial executive function scores, who completed the mindfulness based program, showed gains in behavioral regulation, meta-cognition, and overall global executive control. These results indicate that mindfulness-based training can benefit children with executive function difficulties.

A study conducted with $4^{th}$-$7^{th}$ graders and their parents showed that after 75 mintues of mindfulness training for 8 consecutive weeks, the children demonstrated increased ability to orient their attention (as measured by the objective computer-based Attention Network Task) and decreased anxiety (Saltzman and Goldin, 2008). Semple et al. (2010) offered a manualized group therapy, developed specifically to increase social-emotional resiliency through the enhancement of mindful attention, to 25 boys and girls aged 9-13 mostly from low-income, inner-city households. Participants who completed the program showed fewer attention problems than those in the control group, and these improvements were maintained at three months following the inter=vention. This study also identified a strong relationship between attention problems and behavior problems, and reductions in attention problems accounted for 46% of the variance of changes in behavior problems.

Another study showed mindfulness training significantly reduced emotional and social problems among low-income minority children (Lee et al., 2008). Mindfulness programs have also been tailored to students with learning disabilities such as ADHD, autism, and those with academic difficulties. Taken together, these studies suggest that mindfulness training has the potential to improve students' attentional skills and compliant behavior, and reduce aggression (Singh et al., 2008; Singh et al., 2007; Singh et al., 2010; Zylowska et al., 2008).

In a RCT with over 100 adolescents, Biegel et al. (2009) found MBSR reduced symptoms of anxiety, depression, and somatic distress, and increased self-esteem and sleep quality. Liehr and Diaz (2010) showed that ethnically diverse children who participated in mindfulness classes reported a reduction in depressive symptoms. Other studies also have found that mindfulness training is associated with decreases in aggressive behaviors, problem behaviors, and increases in attention and concentration, socio-emotional competence, and academic performance (Beauchemin, Hutchins and Patterson, 2008; Schonert-Reichl and Lawlor, 2010). These results and ongoing research into mindfulness as a foundation for Stress Ed likely will encourage more schools to incorporate mindfulness into their curricula to enhance students' attention, learning, pro-social behavior, mental health and well-being.

## STRESS ED FOR SCHOOL STAFF

Many school staff who are exposed to mindfulness via programs offered to students by outside providers become interested in learning mindfulness to reduce their own stress and enhance their well-being. Research on programs such as SMART[8], CARE[9], and the Inner-Resilience program[10] has demonstrated that school staff who practice mindfulness reap the benefits documented in the general adult population: decreased stress, compassion-fatigue and burn-out, and enhanced job satisfaction, empathy, and efficacy. Many of these school staff come full circle; after experiencing the benefits of mindfulness in their own lives, they are even more inspired to incorporate mindfulness into their daily classroom routines. Programs that offer mindfulness to school staff are now beginning to partner with the programs that offer mindfulness to students.

Over the next 5-10 years, the practice of mindfulness likely will be increasingly incorporated into teacher and counselor degree programs, continuing education programs, as well as K-12 school curricula. Some forward-thinking counselor and teacher degree programs already are integrating personal adult mindfulness training into their standard curricula in order to prepare their graduates for the stressors of their chosen profession.[11] Over time, the combined effects of staff and student Stress Ed curricula will likely have significant benefits such as decreasing staff burnout and compassion fatigue, and increasing staff empathy and effectiveness, while decreasing student self-destructive behavior, and improving student attention, learning, mental health, and interpersonal relations. As indicated earier in this

[8] http://www.smart-in-education.org

[9] http://www.garrisoninstitute.org/index.php?option=com_content&view=article&id=143:garrisons-institutes-care-program-for-teachers-receives-federal-funding&catid=108&Itemid=59

[10] http://www.innerresilience-tidescenter.org/evaluations.html

[11] http://www.geoffreysoloway.com/Research.html

section, emerging research suggests that these outcomes are within reach. Although, momentum is growing to incorporate mindfulness into school setting for the health and well being of both students and staff, barriers exist for those interested in incorporating mindfulness based Stress Ed into standard curricula. Next, we discuss these barriers along with potential solutions.

## Barriers and Solutions to Implementing Mindfulness-Based Stress Ed in Schools

Several barriers exist to incoporating mindfulness-based Stress Ed into schools. The central barrier is awareness. Many counselors and teachers are not yet aware of mindfulness and its documented benefits. However, the growing number of research articles, review articles, and educational conferences will continue to increase awareness of the benefits of mindfulness- based Stress Ed among teachers and school staff. A second barrier is resistance to incorporating new curricula, including Stress Ed, into an established school system; however, this issue is likely to be overcome as scientific evidence accumulates and teachers are informed about the benefits of mindfulness programs. A third barrier is resistance by parents, teachers, or administrators who confuse mindfulness with religion and esoteric practice. This barrier is most easily overcome by offering educational sessions before starting the program. Educations sessions typically include an explanation of secular mindfulness-based Stress Ed program, a brief practice where participants can experience their own natural capacity for mindfulness, a review of the current research, and time for questions and answers.

Ironically, another barrier is that many well-intentioned and devoted individuals within our school systems are simply scrambling to support too many students with too little time and too few resources. While systemic issues definitely need to be addressed, counselors and teachers who practice mindfulness are less likely to feel overwhelmed and more likely to have the individual and collective resources to initiate new programs. Further, offering students mindfulness-based Stress Ed in large groups, and equipping them with essential life skills for working with intense emotions, dealing with challenges and making healthy choices, may reduce the number of students who need intensive individual support, which in turn will decrease the demands placed on school staff. Two additional challenges exist. As more schools wish to incorporate mindfulness into the curricula, there may be a shortage of experienced instructors. For students to reap the benefits documented in the research, mindfulness courses must be offered by trained staff who have an established daily mindfulness practice. As with counseling, the self-reflective nature of mindfulness may result in students acknowledging sensitive emotional and psychological issues, which must be handled with extreme care. A brief weekend workshop is unlikely to provide the depth of training needed to skillfully address the sensitive issues that may arise when working with students. Thus, schools need to promote daily mindfulness practice for those interested in offering youth mindfulness-based Stress Ed. Quality training programs, like those mentioned earlier in this chapter, can help address this challenge. Finally, probably the greatest challenge to incorporating mindfulness into school curricula is funding. With the current economic crisis, many support programs and counseling positions are being cut. These financial pressures suggest that it is even more crucial to offer essential skills to all students in a cost effective manner. Eventually, we hope that field of education evolves so that the majority counselor- and teacher-training incorportates mindfulness practices in order to address the stress in the lives of school faculty and their students. Until the field evolves accordingly, opportunities for program funding include research grants, professional development grants, community grants, PTO and PTA grants, individual “angel” grants, pro bono provision of services, and individual donations and time-commitments from counselors and teachers.

## CONCLUSION

As socializing institutions, schools need to address the psychological stress faced by children and adolescents. Our nation’s youth suffer from psychological ailments at rates that are embarrassing to admit, and shameful to leave unaddressed. To address these issues, this chapter presented the concept of mindfulness-based Stress Ed, which is a curriculum created to help youth in schools and other contexts develop internal resources to combat everyday stressors and thrive during their years of school, and also throughout their lives. If youth can deal with stressors as they arise, it is less likely that they will have long-lasting stress-related problems later in life. Schools are the most efficient setting to deliver such mindfulness-based Stress Ed programming. But broad implementation of such programming has its challenges in areas of personnel, buy-in, school climate, and funding levels. As evidence continues to accumulate regarding the benefits of mindfulness-based Stress Ed programs, and as teachers, school leaders, and policy makers become more aware of the benefits of Stress Ed, these challenges are likely to be surmounted. Ultimately, our nations' youth will be the greatest beneficiaries of these efforts.

## References

Alexander-Passe, N. (2008). The sources and manifestations of stress amongst school-aged dyslexics, compared with sibling controls. *Dyslexia*, *14*(4), 291-313.

Anisman, H. and Matheson, K. (2005). Stress, depression, and anhedonia: Caveats concerning animal models. *Neuroscience and Biobehavioral Reviews*, *29* (4-5), 525.

Beauchemin, J., Hutchins, T. L., and Patterson, F. (2008). Mindfulness meditation may lessen anxiety, promote social skills, and improve academic performance among adolescents with learning disabilities. *Complementary Health Practice Review*, *13*(1), 34-45.

Bender, W. N., Rosenkrans, C. B., and Crane, M. K. (1999). Stress, depression, and suicide among students with learning disabilities: Assessing the risk. *Learning Disability Quarterly*, *22*(2), 143-156.

Biegel, G. M., Brown, K. W., Shapiro, S. L., and Schubert, C. M. (2009). Mindfulness-Based stress reduction for the treatment of adolescent psychiatric outpatients: A randomized clinical trial. *Journal of Consulting and Clinical Psychology*, *77*(5), 855-66.

Blum, R. W., Beuhring, T., Shew, M. L., Bearinger, L. H., Sieving, R. E., and Resnick, M. D. (2000). The effects of race/ethnicity, income, and family structure on adolescent risk behaviors. *American Journal of Public Health*, *90*(12), 1879.

Bogard, K. L. (2005). Affluent adolescents, depression, and drug use: The role of adults in their lives. *Adolescence*, *40*(158), 281.

Bos, K. J., Fox, N., Zeanah, C. H., and Nelson III, C. A. (2009). Effects of early psychosocial deprivation on the development of memory and executive function. *Frontiers in Behavioral Neuroscience*, *3*(16), 1-7.

Chambers, R., Lo, B. C. Y., and Allen, N. B. (2008). The impact of intensive mindfulness training on attentional control, cognitive style, and affect. *Cognitive Therapy and Research*, *32*(3), 303-322.

Colvert, E., Rutter, M., Kreppner, J., Beckett, C., Castle, J., Groothues, C., et al. (2008). Do theory of mind and executive function deficits underlie the adverse outcomes associated with profound early deprivation?: Findings from the English and romanian adoptees study. *Journal of Abnormal Child Psychology*, *36*(7), 1057.

Copeland, W. E., Keeler, G., Angold, A., and Costello, E. J. (2007). Traumatic events and posttraumatic stress in childhood. *Archives of General Psychiatry*, *64*(5), 577-84.

Cuijpers, P. (2002). Effective ingredients of school-based drug prevention programs. A systematic review. *Addictive Behaviors*, *27*(6), 1009-23.

Elder, R. W., Nichols, J. L., Shults, R. A., Sleet, D. A., Barrios, L. C., and Compton, R. (2005). Effectiveness of school-based programs for reducing drinking and driving and riding with drinking drivers: A systematic review. *American Journal of Preventive Medicine*, *28*(S5), 288.

Evans, G. W. and Schamberg, M. A. (2009). Childhood poverty, chronic stress, and adult working memory. *Proceedings of the National Academy of Sciences of the United States of America*, *106*(16), 6545-49.

Flook, L., Smalley, S. L., Kitil, M. J., Galla, B. M., Kaiser-Greenland, S., Locke, J., et al. (2010). Effects of mindful awareness practices on executive functions in elementary school children. *Journal of Applied School Psychology*, *26*(1), 70-95.

Frodl, T., Reinhold, E., Koutsouleris, N., Donohoe, G., Bondy, B., Reiser, M., et al. (2010). Childhood stress, serotonin transporter gene and brain structures in major depression. *Neuropsychopharmacology*, *35*(6), 1383-90.

Geisthardt, C. and Munsch, J. (1996). Coping with school stress: A comparison of adolescents with and without learning disabilities. *Journal of Learning Disabilities*, *29*(3), 287-96.

Kabat-Zinn, J. (1982). An outpatient program in behavioral medicine for chronic pain patients based on the practice of mindfulness meditation: Theoretical considerations and preliminary results. *General Hospital Psychiatry*, *4*(1), 33-47.

Kabat-Zinn, J., Lipworth, L., and Burney, R. (1985). The clinical use of mindfulness meditation for the self-regulation of chronic pain. *Journal of Behavioral Medicine*, *8*(2), 163-90.

Kabat-Zinn, J., Lipworth, L., Burncy, R., and Sellers, W. (1986). Four-Year follow-up of a meditation-based program for the self-regulation of chronic pain: Treatment outcomes and compliance. *Clinical Journal of Pain*, *2*(3), 159.

Kabat-Zinn, J., Massion, A. O., Kristeller, J., Peterson, L. G., Fletcher, K. E., Pbert, L., et al. (1992). Effectiveness of a meditation-based stress reduction program in the treatment of anxiety disorders. *The American Journal of Psychiatry*, *149*(7), 936-43.

Kirby, D., Short, L., Collins, J., Rugg, D., Kolbe, L., Howard, M., et al. (1994). School-Based programs to reduce sexual risk behaviors: A review of effectiveness. *Public Health Reports*, *109*(3), 339-60.

Lee, J., Semple, R. J., Rosa, D., and Miller, L. (2008). Mindfulness-Based cognitive therapy for children: Results of a pilot study. *Journal of Cognitive Psychotherapy*, *22*(1), 15-28.

Leung, C. and To, H. (2009). The relationship between stress and bullying among secondary school students. *New Horizons in Education*, *57*(1), 10.

Liehr, P. and Diaz, N. (2010). A pilot study examining the effect of mindfulness on depression and anxiety for minority children. *Archives of Psychiatric Nursing*, *24*(1), 69-71.

Luthar, S. (2003). The culture of affluence: the psychological costs of material wealth. *Child Development*, *74*(6), 1581-93.

Luthar, S. S. and D'Avanzo, K. (1999). Contextual factors in substance use: A study of suburban and inner-city adolescents. *Development and Psychopathology*, *11*(4), 845-67.

Maag, J. W. and Reid, R. (2006). Depression among students with learning disabilities. *Journal of Learning Disabilities*, *39*(1), 3-10.

Majer, M., Nater, U. M., Lin, J. M. S., Capuron, L., and Reeves, W. C. (2010). Association of childhood trauma with cognitive function in healthy adults: A pilot study. *BMC Neurology*, *10*,61.

Middlebrooks, J. S. and Audage, N. C. (2008). The effects of childhood stress on health across the lifespan. Atlanta, GA: Centers for disease control and prevention. *National Center for Injury Prevention and Control.*

Napoli, M. (2004). Mindfulness training for teachers: A pilot program. *Complementary Health Practice Review*, *9*(1), 31-42.

Pechtel, P. and Pizzagalli, D. A. (2011). Effects of early life stress on cognitive and affective function: An integrated review of human literature. *Psychopharmacology*, *214*(1), 55-70.

Saltzman, A. and Goldin, P. (2008). Mindfulness based stress reduction for school-age children. In *In L. Grecco. Acceptance and mindfulness interventions for children and adolescents: A practitioner's guide.* Oakland: New Harbinger.

Schonert-Reichl, K. A. and Lawlor, M. S. (2010). The effects of a mindfulness-based education program on pre-and early adolescents' well-being and social and emotional competence. *Mindfulness*, *1*(3), 137-51.

Semple, R. J., Lee, J., Rosa, D., and Miller, L. F. (2010). A randomized trial of mindfulness-based cognitive therapy for children: Promoting mindful attention to enhance social-emotional resiliency in children. *Journal of Child and Family Studies*, *19*(2), 218-229.

Shapiro, S. L., Schwartz, G. E., and Bonner, G. (1998). Effects of mindfulness-based stress reduction on medical and premedical students. *Journal of Behavioral Medicine*, *21*(6), 581-99.

Simpson, G. A., Bloom, B., Cohen, R. A., Blumberg, S., and Bourdon, K. H. (2005). US children with emotional and behavioral difficulties: Data from the 2001, 2002, and 2003 national health interview surveys. *Advance Data*, (360), 1-13.

Singh, N. N., Lancioni, G. E., Singh, A. N., Winton, A. S., Singh, J., McAleavey, K. M., et al. (2008). A mindfulness-based health wellness program for an adolescent with prader-willi syndrome. *Behavior Modification*, *32*(2), 167-81.

Singh, N. N., Lancioni, G. E., Singh Joy, S. D., Winton, A. S. W., Sabaawi, M., Wahler, R. G., et al. (2007). Adolescents with conduct disorder can be mindful of their aggressive behavior. *Journal of Emotional and Behavioral Disorders*, *15*(1), 56-63.

Singh, N. N., Singh, A. N., Lancioni, G. E., Singh, J., Winton, A. S. W., and Adkins, A. D. (2010). Mindfulness training for parents and their children with ADHD increases the children's compliance. *Journal of Child and Family Studies*, *19*(2), 157-166.

Weber, K., Rockstroh, B., Borgelt, J., Awiszus, B., Popov, T., Hoffmann, K., et al. (2008). Stress load during childhood affects psychopathology in psychiatric patients. *BMC Psychiatry*, *8*, 63.

Zylowska, L., Ackerman, D. L., Yang, M. H., Futrell, J. L., Horton, N. L., Hale, T. S., et al. (2008). Mindfulness meditation training in adults and adolescents with ADHD: A feasibility study. *Journal of Attention Disorders*, *11*(6), 737-46.

In: Child and School Psychology ISBN: 978-1-61470-801-8
Editors: M. Haines et al., pp. 125-143 

*Chapter 5*

# MULTI-DISCIPLINARY* TEAMWORK IN SPECIAL EDUCATION SCHOOL– ETHNOGRAPHIC TRIANGLE

***Iris Manor-Binyamini***
University of Haifa, Haifa, Israel

## ABSTRACT

In recent decades both researchers and professionals agree that inter-disciplinary team collaboration has become a particularly important component of work planning and implementation in inclusive and special education schools. Collaboration inter-disciplinary teamwork is a vibrant realm of social processes and complex framework of activity. This study examines and analyzes how collaborative Collaboration inter-disciplinary teamwork in a special education school takes place in everyday life. This is ethnographic case study which examines the activities of 65 members of an inter-disciplinary team: educators, therapist and physicians working in collaboration in a special education school. Data was gathered through observations (formal and informal) of inter-disciplinary team meetings, individual interviews and document collection during one year of research.

Analysis of the data indicates that Collaboration is based on three components: contents, structures and processes. This component is examined with respect to Collaboration objectives. The uniqueness of this research lies in the understanding and presentation of the complexity of the functioning of an multi -disciplinary team in daily life. Data findings may be utilized as a conceptual platform for research and professionals in the field in examining additional question and may also serve as the basis for designing applies tools for working with multi-disciplinary team in education in general and in special education in particular.

- I use the terms Multi-Disciplinary and Inter-disciplinary interchangeably

# INTRODUCTION

The need for multi-disciplinary work in the social sciences has gained recognition and developed considerably in recent years in various fields such as: education, health, sociology, organizations, welfare, economic development and research (Secker and Hill, 2001), and also in the field of special education. In this field, as in other fields of specialization, researchers found that a single profession or discipline is unable to provide good solutions to the complicated problems arising in the field. Therefore the inter-disciplinary approach was considered to be the best solution for the problems: instead of the specialized professional approach, the preferred approach today is the integration of most of the relevant fields that lead to collaboration action, leading to an effective solution. This is the reason behind the fact that the supporting services are encouraged to develop multi-disciplinary work. The main supporting service for work with children with complex special needs (such as moderate and severe intellectual disability, autism with low functioning, behavioral disturbances, etc.) and children with multiple disorders,(such as autism and mental retardation), are the special education schools in which multi-disciplinary teams are active on a daily basis. In Israel these teams are subject to the Law of Special Education (1988). The profession of special education serves as an "anchor profession" in the multi-disciplinary work, namely the work of the various professional workers is conducted within the school – a defined location in which special education, combined with other professions, create multi-professional activity under the leadership of the profession of special education. Each one of the related disciplines developed its own specialized theories that were tested in a separate and restricted framework. As a result, differentiated concepts and values for every field of knowledge were developed over the years, namely professional language and culture, patterns of action, practical knowledge resulting from experience in the field, research tools and training methods. The fact that disciplinary thinking is rooted in the delineation of its boundaries, is the source of both its strength and its weakness, since most social phenomena are more complex than any of the professional fields dealing with them. Therefore, in order to deal effectively with complex phenomena/ problems, several fields of knowledge must be involved simultaneously. This constitutes both the professional challenge and the focus of difficulty at one and the same time.

This policy is based on a rationale containing eight main arguments:

First, The most common argument in favor of a multi-disciplinary team is based on the fact that solutions to complex problems require a wide spectrum of knowledge and abilities (Payne, 2000; Heinemann, 2002), namely responding to the unique needs of a pupil with complex and/or multiple disorders in a school for special education, requires expertise in more than one field of knowledge; in educational systems this can be achieved only by efficient team work. Practical considerations also indicate the added value of multi-disciplinary work, for instance: in situations in which there is a feeling of a lack of knowledge and/or lack of success in dealing with complex problems by professionals specializing in one field. Multi-disciplinary work can enable a new and different look at the reality situation and also the identification of new opportunities for activity (Lasker and Weiss, 2003). There is a need to adjust new ways of dealing with a social reality which is becoming more complex from day to day. Moreover, the combination of ideas and professional approaches, not combined so far, can bring about a new breakthrough.

Second, a variety of professional abilities and the sharing of knowledge are considered necessary conditions for a holistic approach to the pupil. The condition for the development of a pupil is a holistic approach to his needs, namely looking at him in developmental, academic, functional, social, emotional, behavioral and family contexts. This way of looking at him is quite different from that of professionals working in one field of specialization, which enables only a partial representation of the pupil ( Proctor, Child, Freeman and Miller, 1998).

Third, social changes have brought about greater appreciation for the "satisfaction of the client" in the support services. Calnan and his associates (Calnan, Cant, Williams and Killoran, 1994) define satisfaction not only in terms of measurable outputs, but also as a factor capable of affecting the readiness of the client to accept support services. Research comparing the results of inter-disciplinary work with those of multi-disciplinary work is rather scarce in the literature. Nevertheless, higher levels of satisfaction with support services offered by a multi-disciplinary team have been reported

(Carlsson, 2001; Lowe and O`Hara, 2000; Colombo et. al, 2003; Pearson and Spencer, 1995).

Fourth, another argument worth considering is that more effective learning takes place if the professional team members have received training in multi-disciplinary skills (Littlewood, 1988). Learning is facilitated by means of shared consultations between team members: every specialist has an opportunity of broadening his knowledge and understanding in another field of expertise and understands better where his expertise can combine with that of another expert. Multi-disciplinary work in special education can be carried out in different forms and incorporate a variety of participants in a variety of fields of expertise – educators, occupational therapists, speech therapists, social workers, teachers, doctors and psychologists.

Fifth, all the subjects that specialists/teams deal with in schools for special education – defining the program of work, quality of education-treatment, work methods, etc. are relevant to the work of the team. If the work of the team members is not adjusted to life at school, the pupil`s progress cannot be successfully promoted. In other words, such systematic and consistent work helps the pupil to progress because it saves time and effort of the professionals involved. Team work enables them to limit the number of repetitions and congruences to which the pupil would be exposed if they were to work separately. It also enables continuity and flow of work: if, for instance, all those concerned would plan together how to deal with his problems, it would improve the quantity and quality of "work time" that the pupils could receive (Fleming, 2000). Such work enables the child with special needs to receive the greatest benefit from the help given to him.

Sixth, multi-disciplinary work is becoming more and more in demand in modern society. This development is the result of increasing specialization of the support services and the growing number of experts involved in their work (Bihari-Axelsson and Axelsson, 2009). The process of fragmentation of the various disciplines is integrated with the tendency towards professional specialization and this constitutes a major characteristic of the modern era, as a result of the immense increase in the quantity of knowledge and information and the complexity of the problems of modern societies. Therefore the only way to gain a broad perspective in dealing with complex situations, is to create links between the various fields of knowledge (Nissani, 2005). It is unrealistic to expect us to be experts in all the dimensions of the issues that we are dealing with. In order to obtain a full picture we must work in a multi - disciplinary team.

Seventh, there seems to be a conceptual confusion concerning concepts involved in the work of a multi-disciplinary team. The literature contains many different concepts, some of them contradictory, such as networks, partnerships, coalition, co-ordination, co-operation and collaboration (Grone and Garcia-Barbero, 2002). Moreover, the theoretical relation between these concepts and others is not always clear; this lies in the nature of a relatively new field of research (Bihari-Axelsson and Axelsson, 2009) – inter-professional practice, inter-professional collaboration, collaboration, inter-disciplinary practice, multidisciplinary teams, trans-professional practice, teams, teamwork (are a few examples of such concepts).

The work between the specialists in a school for special education is organized in the form of an multi-disciplinary team. This can be defined as a small group of persons from different fields of expertise, working together across formal organizational boundaries in order to provide services to the pupils. Huxham says that "Working together with (the) other is never simple, but when collaboration is across boundaries the complications are magnified" (Huxham, 1996).

On the basis of what was said in this review I would like to offer the following definition of the term "multi-disciplinary team": The work of the multi-disciplinary team is intended to help in coping with simple to complicated issues and problems of pupils with special needs on the school level, by means of applied activity - integrating different fields of knowledge - as required by the nature of the information, the problem or the issue dealt with. These are long-term connections between experts in a number of fields producing work leading to new ways of action with synergetic results, beyond those common in actions deriving from separate fields of knowledge or from links between fields. This approach integrates processes of action and processes of learning and leads to the empowerment of individuals and groups towards effective work and progress of the pupil with special needs.

The definition presented contains three significant components in the work of schools for special education:

1. Long-term multi-disciplinary work – namely, orderly and continuous cooperation between relevant professionals (working with the pupil).
2. Concentrating on complex issues or multiple-disorders deficiency.
3. Synergetic result – the result of such involvement is considered more effective than the sum of work in different fields, carried out separately.

Eighth, such work encounters structural, legislative and administrative barriers which are difficult to cross. Other barriers are the result of cultural differences between experts and organizations, for instance: a particular language (Manor-Binyamini, 2007), difference in values and in relating – all these impede communication and cooperation. This orientation towards barriers and difficulties led to a negative and pessimistic point of view concerning the multi-disciplinary approach and other kinds of cooperation (Bihari-Axelsson and Axelsson, 2009). Every field of knowledge has its own perspective and professional ethic – by the term perspective I mean, the point of view we adopt in examining reality. That means that a person who has internalized a certain field of knowledge has not only acquired a set of facts in this field but mainly a certain way of understanding the world and acting in it.

Taking the above into consideration, multi-disciplinary work is considered a right and effective way to achieve goals for pupils with special needs. In spite of the importance of multi-disciplinary work on a daily basis, there is still a large gap between declarations concerning the importance of such work and the practical application in the field, namely in schools for special education (Detmer et.al.2005), or as Zwarenstein argues "What`s so great about collaboration? we need more evidence and less rhetoric" (Zwarenstein and Reeves, 2000, p.1022). Moreover, the work of multi-disciplinary teams has not been studied systematically (McCallin, 2000). Studies explaining how members of multi-disciplinary teams carry out their work in practice are extremely scarce (McCallin, 2000). What is important, he says, is what these teams do and how they do it. In an attempt to bridge the gap between rhetoric and practical application, I will present an applied model demonstrating the practical work of a multi-disciplinary team.

The model presented in this chapter is based on an ethnographic study, because ethnography enables us to expose the nature of the work of the multi-disciplinary team in the everyday life of the school.

While the number of studies focusing on the work of multi-disciplinary teams has increased continuously, the understanding and research of this phenomenon has been limited by two characteristics of the literature. First, a number of studies only collected data from interviews (Reeves et al., 2009). Such an approach enables us to receive a first-hand report of experts on their work in cooperation with others, but the question remains concerning their capacity to describe their work as it was carried out in reality, accurately (Reeves et al, 2009). The limited number of studies containing observations of multi-disciplinary teams shows that this type of activity was extremely dependent on informal interaction between the experts (Cott, 1998: Ellingson,

2003) and this creates difficulties in understanding the work of the multi-disciplinary team. This chapter focuses on formal continuous and permanent staff meetings.

Second, studies conducted in the field did not enable the development of a theory on the basis of their findings. As a result, our knowledge concerning the work of a multi-disciplinary team usually remained on the level termed by Mills (1967) "abstracted empiricism" – work that fails to be informed by relevant theoretical explanation which can enhance our understanding of the phenomenon under study". This study exposes the nature of inter-disciplinary team work that occurs within a special education school. It uses ethnographic methods to generate a rich account of their daily life in school, to provide a lens by which to help illuminate the nature of their work within this context.

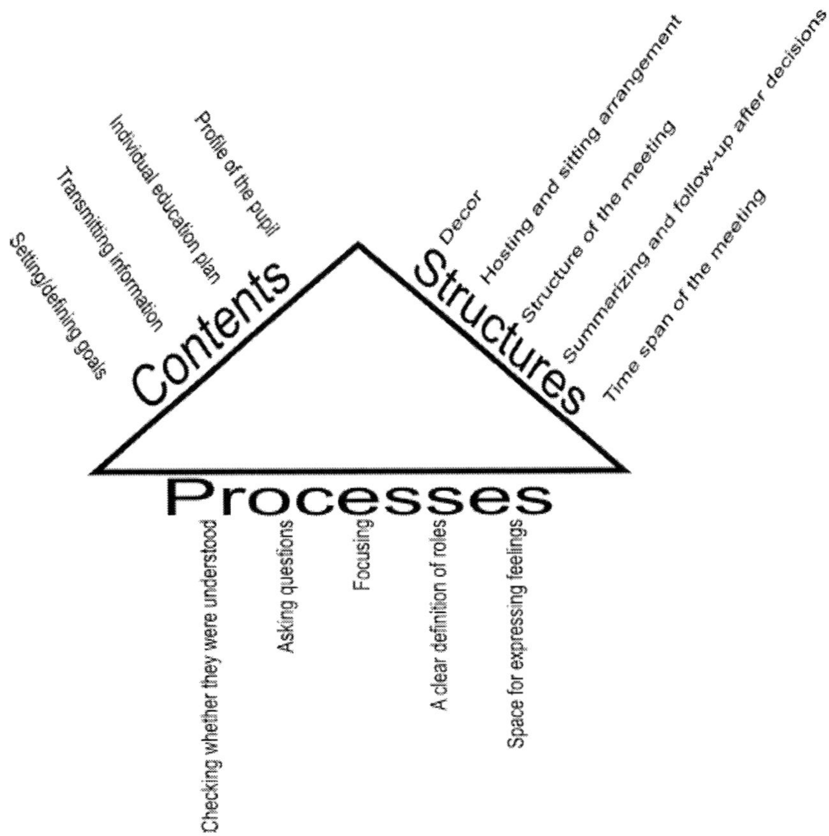


Drawing 1. An ethnographic triangle for the work of a multi-disciplinary team – contents, structures and processes.

## An Ethnographic Triangle for the Work of a Multi-Disciplinary Team – Contents, Structures and Processes

In this section I will present an ethnographic triangle. The triangle is based on my one-year study of the work of a multi-disciplinary team in a school for children with moderate and severe intellectual disability pupil in the age of 7 – 21 - and on interviews conducted with members of the team throughout the year. I will first present the model and after that a detailed description of its components.

## CONTENTS

This part contains the following components: profile of the pupil, individual education plan, transmitting information, setting/defining goals.

### Profile of the Pupil

The profile of the pupil is a comprehensive picture which the members of the team produce together for each pupil in the school. The profile constitutes the basis for preparing the individual education plan for each pupil. The profile, the points of strength and the points to be strengthened in various areas include: learning, social, emotional, behavioral, communicative, function and cognitive areas. In addition' observations show that the teams relate to the following three components as a matter of course: a. the educational policy of the school, b. the inclinations of the pupil and c. the requests of the parents.

### Individual Education Plan

The individual education plan (IEP) is discussed three times throughout the year, at the beginning of the year, in the middle and in the end. In all meetings of the IEP for every pupil, the following characteristics were found: the multi-disciplinary team adapts the IEP to the individual needs of the pupil, the team involves the parents and the pupil, the IEP is oriented to work with the educators, the teachers and the therapists, the IEP includes areas of learning, treatment and other activities and is relevant to the present state of the pupil, his future in the educational setting and his age.

It is dynamic, namely changes according to the growing familiarity with the pupil, evaluation findings and feed-back by the members of the team working with him. The IEP has a fixed structure and serves as a basis for individual and group work and it documents the planning of long-term work with the pupil.

## Transmitting Information

The main component in transmitting information in the multi-disciplinary team is the use of positive language. Such positive language has several characteristics as observed in formal and informal meetings of the multi-disciplinary teamwork.

The primary characteristic is that positive language is not judgmental or critical. The absence of blaming or criticism conveys a hidden message that the aim of the meeting is to focus on the subject discussed, for example – the pupil and his needs.

Another characteristic is the wording chosen by the professionals: they always formulate their comments in a structured way, starting with a positive description, as, for example: emphasizing the strong points of the pupil throughout the meeting. It is important to mention that what characterizes the work of the team members observed is that they do not shy away from reporting and discussing charged topics. Moreover, they are extremely clear and direct in their descriptions, such as: difficulties encountered by the pupil. All the members of the team mentioned this in the interviews and emphasized that sincerity in transmitting information concerning the deficiencies is essential because it constitutes the basis of trust. Moreover, the professionals express their concern directly. The tone and the body language transmit a message of concern to the other team members.

## Setting/Defining Goals

The goals set by the multi-disciplinary team are long-term and short-term goals in various fields including behavioral, emotional and academic fields and ranking them according to their importance for work with the pupil. In case episodes occur such as, for instance, a behavioral episode, the goals and the way they are treated are oriented toward the pupil and teamwork.

## STRUCTURES

This section includes the following components: decor, hosting and sitting arrangement, structure of the meeting, summarizing and follow-up after decisions are reached, and time span of the meeting. Below are the details of each component:

### Décor

The décor in the school includes physical and additional background details. The physical setting is the room where the meeting takes place and the background details are the furnishing and decoration of the room. According to Goffman (Goffman, 1959), the stage and the accessories on which, in which or inside which, interaction between the members of the multi-disciplinary team takes place. The room designed for meetings of team members and the place where all the meetings are held, is the teachers` room. This room contains plants, easy chairs and many windows and produces a feeling of warmth and comfort for the person entering. The décor in the meeting room was observed to be an important component of the success of the meeting.

### Hosting and Sitting Arrangements

The behavior of the teams was pleasant and relaxed. The members of the team reported in the interviews that the relaxed atmosphere was important as a setting for a positive meeting. Often team members prepare hot drinks in the course of the meeting and there are refreshments on the table. People sometimes eat in the course of the meeting. The food creates a sense of "home" for the participants. The seating pattern in all the meetings is in a circle. The circle enables all the participants to see each other, to talk face to face and create a feeling of intimacy.

### Structure of the Meeting

In all meetings observed the structure of the meeting was fixed and repetitive. This structure included: opening-discussion-closing the meeting.

*Opening* – the meeting usually begins with questions that arose in the previous meeting of the team and sometimes with events that occurred at school in the morning, such as: the state of a pupil who had experienced a severe outburst in class.

*Discussion* – Many topics are presented and discussed in the course of the multi-disciplinary meeting. There is also an internal structure of the proceedings at the meetings. The order observed is the following and I will present one example of meetings concerning a pupil: conveying relevant information about the diagnosis/evaluation of the pupil, background information, in this way, for example in the IEP meetings – a holistic profile of the pupil, in which the professionals impart information about the pupil in various areas, including: developmental, learning, emotional, social and academic, was presented. A clear profile of the pupil is produced by all the professionals. Referral to continuation of diagnosis or reaching shared decisions concerning a program of treatment/involvement. They present the topics along with information derived from various fields of knowledge to produce a whole picture.

*Closing the meeting* – Presenting the decisions reached in the course of the meeting

## Summary and Follow up of the Decisions

Every meeting was documented by one of the professionals and the protocols were then printed. In the course of some of the meetings decisions on various topics and areas were reached, such as referring a pupil to a neurologist, determining the method of work with the pupil.

At the end of every meeting one of the team members summarized and integrated the information imparted in the course of the meeting. This is especially important in multi-disciplinary meetings since a great deal of information is imparted. A professional, not formally entrusted with this role, does the integration. This summary enables the teams to reach decisions. In every one of the teams the summary of the decisions is distributed once in a month, with copies to all the professionals expected to follow up the decisions.

In most cases the following meeting of the team begins with reference to the decisions reached at the previous meeting.

### Time Span of the Meeting

Many professionals participate in the multi-disciplinary meetings and many topics are discussed and dealt with. Therefore it is quite surprising that all the meetings of the teams observed in the course of the year were terminated at a fixed time. Keeping the time schedule was made possible because the team members were focused. Each one of them in his turn, ommunicated his information to the rest of the members in a clear and organized fashion. In the interviews the professionals mentioned the importance of adhering to the aims of the meeting. According to their opinion, this way of working is effective.

## PROCESSES

This section includes the following components: checking whether they were understood, asking questions, focusing, clear definition of roles, space for expressing feelings, communication, making decision and explaining professional terminology. A detailed description of the components is as follows:

### Checking Whether They Were Understood

Whenever the professionals imparted information to each other, they often checked to see whether they were understood correctly. They did so by watching the other members and evaluated the situation in a non-verbal way and also by asking direct questions or waiting for a response. The analysis of the interviews shows that they regarded this strategy as a good way of fostering cooperation.

## Asking Questions

The team members ask many questions in the course of the meeting. This activity seems to be another way of validating their statements and those of their partners in the team. The questions asked fall into two categories: one is questions requesting details or specific examples of behaviors or ways of learning/treating a pupil, and the other – questions requesting an opinion from other team members.

In most of the meetings a gradual passage of professionals from open questions, asked at the beginning of the meeting, to focused questions at the end. Observations conducted on the team show clearly that the more confident the team members feel, the freer they feel to ask questions in the course of the meetings. Asking questions enables the professionals to participate in the discourse in the meeting. It also helps to raise new ideas and resolve problems. The questions help to clarify matters and focus on problems.

## Focusing

Observations show that the capacity to conduct multi-disciplinary meetings with a large number of participants and to promote work with the pupil and encourage multi-disciplinary thinking, are based on the serious attitude of the participants to the meeting and to the work being done there. As the professionals defined it in the meetings, all the professionals arrive prepared for the meetings, i.e. they are acquainted with the pupils and the topics discussed, as the psychiatrist in interview defines it:

> "Look, there are very good professionals here, all of them, really all, come prepared to the meetings, they know all the pupils, the strengths and weaknesses of every one of them and the goals of the work with them"

The acquaintance of the professional worker enables the members to listen to him because he does not have to plan what he is going to say or study his documents. Thus he can direct his attention to his colleagues at the meeting, look at their faces, see if he is understood. This contributes to the flow of the meetings and to focused work.

## A Clear Definition of Roles

The idea of the team members is that every member has an active role to fulfill in the team meetings. The professionals expect their colleagues to be active in the meetings, and regard participation as part of their role. The team members tend to interpret the lack of participation of other professionals in the team as a failure in their functioning, as one of the speech therapists said in her interview:

> "We work really hard to bring all the team members including the paraprofessional to ask questions, express their opinion, present conflicts and difficulties. We always want everybody to be more involved."

A clear definition of roles based on trust or better still, on altruism, was observed to be an essential condition for the work of the multi-disciplinary team. Such an attitude, namely an attempt by the professional to regard the role and assignments of the other in relation to the other fields of expertise, especially to the pupil who is the object of the cooperation, enables the members to cope with territorial conflicts.

It is not easy for the professional to take/perceive/understand this point of view, but in the interviews this issue appeared to be a condition for the work of the multi-disciplinary team. Altruism, according to the professionals, is the ability to regard the work of the professional in another field from a comprehensive and long-term point of view, and the ability to compromise if necessary for the sake of the pupil and the mutual work.

## Space for Expressing Feelings

The members of these teams are ready to allocate place, validity and focus to the feelings of other professionals. If it seems that a professional experienced difficulties or anxiety in his work with a pupil, the team members tend to focus the feelings of the professional and thus make the continuation of the discussion possible.

The professionals speak gently but in a professional way. They look straight in the eyes of the members speaking and listen carefully to their answers. They convey a message that their feelings are important and relevant and often relate to the feelings and questions of other team members.

In contrast, refraining from allocating space for the feelings of a professional by ignoring what he said or assuming a defensive attitude, could cause the professional to distance himself and prevent him from contributing to the meeting.

## Communication

In all the meetings speech was used as the major channel of communication: all the participants interact with one another in a meeting as speaker/sender vs. hearer/receiver of messages.

The type of speech encouraged is relatively a formal one, requiring some prior knowledge of and familiarity with the student, the way of talking at a formal meeting, and sufficient experience with professional jargon, but it seems that the main rule of interaction is turn-taking.

## Making Decisions

Making decisions in a multi-disciplinary team is a process in which overt and covert factors exist simultaneously in the teamwork. In the team observed, the multi-disciplinary power structure was balanced in the process of decision making. The observation showed that in the process the professionals tend to support each other, without any one of them being overbearing, dominating the discussion or compelling the other team members to accept his point of view against their will.

Obviously, in cases in which the participants do not agree, the discussion, rather than power struggles, is the central factor. The discussions are characterized by a desire to learn rather than to prove who is right. The professionals do not regard the conflict as personal and, therefore, do not take offence and respond to the differences of opinion as an opportunity and a challenge for learning. The words of the speech therapist illustrate this point very well:

> "What we do when there are differences of opinion is to regard the difficulty as a challenge and then the contest begins"

## Explaining Professional Terminology

The observed show the professionals are often uncertain and attempt to decide whether to use a professional term in the description of the pupil or to simplify the terms and use a vocabulary that all team members can understand. The professionals do not refrain from using professional terminology, but they make a point of explaining the terms.

This is an informal strategy facilitating communication. Since lack of understanding of professional terminology can interfere with communication. Besides offering explanations, the team members often cite examples for the purpose of explaining. As one of the teachers said:

> "Understanding the professional terms creates better understanding and gives a clearer picture concerning the state of the pupil discussed".

# SUMMARY

In this chapter I try to examine the components of the team work and present those constituting the basis for the work in daily practice. The importance of this attempt, as shown in the ethnographic triangle, incorporates three factors: contents, structural and processes occurring simultaneously, and therefore requires an investment of time and energies (Bihari-Axelsson and Axelsson, 2009).The most important conclusion is that without a focused, planned and goal-oriented effort in each part of the triangle, effective multi-disciplinary work cannot be carried out in a school for special education where the pupil, constitutes the widest and most profound common ground between the various fields of knowledge.

Besides, long time experience is required in order to encourage the professionals to be involved and open to each other`s knowledge and skills and to learn to regard the differences between them as an advantage for team work. Processes of building trust are also important to enable the professionals to take risks, to give up their routine, to resolve conflicts and create mutual ways of work and culture based on the need for cooperation.

In addition, the reason for the gap between the perception of the importance of multi-disciplinary teamwork as presented in the literature, and the difficulties in applying it in the field could possibly be the result of a lack of an operative definition of team work. Perhaps an answer to the question concerning the significance of the application of such work, as done in this chapter, will help to reduce the gap and the rhetoric on this subject.

Finally, I would like to mention that possibly the triangle presented can be of importance for all supportive services working in multi-disciplinary teams and for the care takers of children, such as, for instance teams working with endangered children.

## REFERENCES


Bihari-Axelsson, S. and Axelsson, R. ( 2009). From territoriality to altruism in *interprofessional* collaboration and Leadership. *Journal of Interprofessional care.* 23(4). 320-330.

Calnan, M., Cant, S., Williams, S., and Killoran, a. (1994). Involvement of the primary healt care team in coronary heart disease prevention. *British Journal of General Practice,* 44, 224-228.

Carlsson, S. (2001). *Peivatpraktiserande lakare och psykologer I samverkan.* Goteborg: Goteborg University, Department of Psychology.

Colombo, A., Bendelow, G., Fulford, B., and Williams, S. (2003). Evaluating the influence of implicit models of mental disorder on processes of shared decision making within community-based multi-disciplinary teams/ *Social Science and Medicine,* 56, 1557-1570.

Cott, C. (1998). Structure and meaning in multidisciplinary teamwork. *Sociology of Health and Illness,* 20(6), 848-873.

Dettmer, P., Thurston, L., and Dyck, N. (2005). *Consultation collaboration, and teamwork for student with special needs.* Boston: Pearson.

Ellingson, L. (2003). Interdisciplinary health care teamwork in the clinic backstage. *Journal of Applied Communication Research,* 31(2), 93-117.

Fleming, G.P. (2000). The effects of brainstorming on subsequent problem-solving. Doctoral dissertation, St. Louis University. *Dissertation Abstracts International,* 61, 2804.

Goffman, E. (1959). *The Presentation of Self in Everyday Life.* New York: Doubleday.

Grone, O. and Garcia-Barbero, M.(2002). *Trends in Integrated Care-Reflections on Conceptual Issues.* European Office for Integrated Health Services: Barcelona.

Heinemann, G.D. (2002). Teams in health care settings. In: G. D. Heinemann and A. M. Zeiss (Eds) *Team performance in health care: Assessment and development.* New York: Kluwer Academic/Plenum Publishers.

Huxham, C. (ed). (1996). *Creating Collaborative Advantage.* Sage: London.

Lasker, R. D. and Weiss, E. S. (2003). Broadening participation in community problem solving: A multidisciplinary model to support collaborative practice and research, *Journal of Urban Health,* Vol. 80(1) . 14- 47.

Littlewood, M. (1988). West Derbyshire community mental health team. In: R. Echlin (Ed.), *Community mental health centres/teams:Information pack.* London: GPMH.

Lowe, F., and O`Hara, S. (2000). Multi-disciplinary team working in practice: Managing the transition. *Journal of Interprofessional Care,* 14, 269-279.

Manor-Binyamini, I. (2007).Meaning of Language different between doctors and educators in collaborative discourse. *Journal of Inter-professional Care.* Vol 21. Issue 1. P 31-43.

McCallin, A. (2000). Interdisciplinary practice – a matter of teamwork: An integrated literature review. *Journal of Clinical Nursing,* 10, 419-428.

Mills, W. (1967). *Power, politicsand people: The collected essays of C. Wright Mills.* New York: Oxford University Press.

Nissani, M.(2005). *Interdisciplinarrity: What, where, why?,*Interdisciplinary Studies

Seminar, Wayne State University. http://www.is.wayne.edu/mnissani/ 20302005/ispessay.htm

Nijhuis, BJG ., Reinders-Messelink, H., Olijve, WE, Groothoff, JW., Nakken, H., and Postema, k. (2007). A review of salient elements defining team collaboration in paediatric rehabilitation. *Clinical Rehabilitation.* 21. P 195-211.

Payne, M. (2000). *Teamwork in multiprofessional care.* London: MacMillan Press Ltd.

Pearson, P., and Spencer, J. (1995). Pointers to effective teamwork: Exploring primary care. *Journal of Interprofessional Care,* 9, 131-138.

Proctor-Childs, T., Freeman, M., and Miller, C.(1998). Vision of teamwork: The realities of an interdisciplinary approach. *British Journal of Therapy and Rehabilitation.* 5(12), 616-618, 635.

Reeves, S., Rice, K., Gotlib, L., Miller, K. L., Kenaszchuk, C., and Zwarenstein, M. (2009). Interprofessional interaction, negotiation and non-negotiation on general internal medicine wards. *Journal of Interprofessional Care.* 23(6). 633-645.

Secker, J. and Hill, K.(2001). Broadening the partnership: experiences of working across community agencies. *Journal of Interprofessional Care.* 15. 341-350.

Special Education Law (1988). State of Israel.

Zwarenstein, M. and Reeves, S. (2000). What`s so great about collaboration? : we need more evidence and less rhetoric. *British Medical Journal,* 320(7241), 1022-1023.

In: Child and School Psychology ISBN: 978-1-61470-801-8
Editors: M. Haines et al., pp. 145-162 

*Chapter 6*

# THE PERCEPTIONS OF SPEECH-LANGUAGE THERAPISTS AND AUDIOLOGISTS REGARDING SPEECH AND HEARING SERVICES IN URBAN SPECIAL EDUCATIONAL SCHOOLS KWA-ZULU NATAL: SOUTH AFRICA

***M. Mophosho, A. Mupawose and N. Ramdin***
School of Human and Community Development
University of Witwatersrand, Johannesburg, South Africa

## INTRODUCTION

In South Africa there is an increased demand of therapy services in schools for learners with special education needs (LSEN) as well as a generalised lack of funding and professionals to provide for these services. According to the Executive Objective Summary, KwaZulu-Natal (KZN) as a province is facing similar challenges to those of the country as a whole. The priority areas for social, economic and demographic development include rural development, urban renewal, economic and employment growth, poverty reduction and human resource development (Statistics South Africa, Census 2001). With regards to the role of Speech Language Pathologists (SLPs) and Audiologists in schools for learners with special education needs (LSEN), there is currently no research in the KwaZulu-Natal (KZN) province that has investigated the professional role of the SLP and audiologist, thus it was crucial to conduct the current study. The services provided in terms of demographical information, availability of services, case load information, resources available and needed, as well as intervention and treatment systems that are in place were also described and explored.

Inclusion in South African schools is an emerging concept. Although ideally inclusion suggests that mainstream schools should be able to adapt and accommodate learners with special education needs (LSEN) in their schools, the idea of having "special" schools for learners with special education needs (LSEN) has developed. "Special" schools should be used as resource centres and to cater for the needs of learners with severe learning impairments. South African education within the "special" education setting is thus still in transformation.

The major problem schools for learners with special education needs (LSEN) in learners with special education needs (KZN) are facing is the fact that there are not enough SLPs and audiologists in schools for (LSEN). Thus the purpose of the current study was to create an awareness of the needs as well as describe the role of SLPs and audiologists in schools for learners with special education needs (LSEN) in the province to educators, parents and other professionals involved with dealing with children with communication disorders.

## BACKGROUND: KWAZULU NATAL PROVINCE

KwaZulu-Natal has the highest population in the country, the Census'01 figures reveals that the province's population is more than 8, 4 million. Of these, more than 4, 4 million are female and around 4 million are male. The disability profile is as follows: 32.1% (sight), 20.1% (hearing), 6.5% (Communication, 29.6% (physical), 12.4% (mental and/or intellectual) and 15.7% with emotional disabilities (Census, 2001). According to Statistics South Africa: Prevalence of Disability in South Africa (Census 2001), the total number of disabled persons in KwaZulu-Natal is 470 588, of which 219 685 are male and 250 903 are female. Of the total amount of disabled persons 154 724 have had no schooling, 131 804 have had some schooling and only 32 571 have completed grade 12 (Statistics South Africa: Prevalence of Disability in South Africa, Census 2001). It was suggested that the high proportion of disabled persons with no schooling is due to the disadvantaged position they have experienced as far as access to educational opportunities is concerned. There are currently 64 schools for LSEN across the 11 districts in the province. Majority of which do not go up until the 7th grade (46 out of the 64 schools, i.e. 72%) and very few that go up to the 10th grade (4 out of the 60 schools, i.e.7%).Only 13 out of 64 schools reported having SLPs, 10 out of 64 schools reported having audiologists and 13 out 64 schools reported having a dual qualified SLPs and audiologists. These findings provide useful information on the number of SLPs and audiologists that are available to provide intervention and services in schools for LSEN in the KZN province. The current number of SLPs and audiologists registered with the Health Professional Council South Africa (HPCSA) across the entire country as at the end of 2008 was 1,222.

## Inclusive Education in South Africa

According to the Department of Education (DOE, 2001; 16), inclusive education and training are about acknowledging that all children and youth can learn and that all children and youth need support. In South Africa the educational policies and practices are in signatory to the UN convention in rights of people with disabilities. Walton, Nel, Hugo and Mueller (2009) state that one of the many challenges facing education in post apartheid South Africa is that of realising the constitutional values of equality, freedom from discrimination and the right to basic education for all learners, including those who experience barriers to learning. Under apartheid, learners were not only educated separately according to race, but a separate special education system served those learners with disabilities and impairments (Walton et al., 2009). To address this and bring educational polices and practices in line with international trends of including learners who experience barriers to learning, in general or mainstream classes, South Africa has enacted legislation and formulated policy which establishes an inclusive education system (Walton et al., 2009).

Speech Language Pathologists (SLPs) and audiologists are vital members of the education team especially since language and communication has been identified and acknowledged as a barrier that can cause learning to breakdown (DOE, 2001). These barriers may become even more compounded if intervention is not provided. Because of the vital role that SLPs and audiologists play within the education system, their practice needs to be efficacious and of benefit to the learner with special needs. Optimal treatment however is dependant on many variables such as availability of services, caseload dilemmas as well as resources available.

ASHA (2006), states that the role that a SLP plays in education involves unique contributions to the multidisciplinary team within which the Speech Language Pathologist (SLP) plays. Some of the roles of the SLP involve; explaining the role that language plays in curriculum, assessment, and instruction, as a basis for appropriate program design, explaining the interconnection between spoken and written language, identifying and analyzing existing literature on scientifically based literacy assessment and intervention approaches, assisting in the selection of screening measures, helping to identify systemic patterns of student need with respect to language skills, assisting in the selection of scientifically based literacy intervention, planning for and conduct professional development on the language basis of literacy and learning and interpreting a school's progress in meeting the intervention needs of its students.

Edgar and Rosa-Lugo (2007) conducted a study in Orlando Florida (USA) which focused on the perspectives of SLPs regarding features of the work environment that contributed to and/or hindered recruitment and retention in the public school setting. The results of the study indicated that working with children, school schedule, and the educational setting was the primary reasons for their satisfaction with working in the public school setting. Furthermore, ranked workload, role ambiguity, salary, and caseload were the primary reasons for their dissatisfaction with working in the public school setting.

In KwaZulu Natal (KZN) there is an increased demand of therapy services in schools for learners with special education needs (LSEN) as well as a generalised lack of funding for these services (DOE, 2001). The province also has the highest number of disabled people in the country (Statistics South Africa: Prevalence of Disability in South Africa, Census 2001). Thus it is expected that similar dissatisfactions as highlighted in the study conducted by Edgar and Rosa-Lugo (2007), in terms of salary and caseload which have affected the service delivery model in Orlando, Florida (USA) and may also affect the service delivery model in KZN South Africa.

There is currently no research that has been carried out in KwaZulu Natal investigating the role of the Speech Language Pathologist (SLP) and Audiologist in schools for learners with special education needs (LSEN) thus exploring the current status of the service delivery model. This type of research will be of utmost significance as will serve as an awareness of the current status and the services offered by Speech Language Pathologists

(SLPs) and audiologists in schools for learners with special education needs (LSEN) in the province to professionals who deal with children with communication disorders and their families. The purpose of the current study was to investigate and explore 5 main areas of service delivery such; demographical status of SLPs and audiologists in schools for learners with special education needs (LSEN) in the KZN province, availability of SLP and audiologists in the schools for learners with special education needs (LSEN) in the KwaZulu Natal (KZN) province, a description of the caseload of the SLPs and audiologists, the resources the SLPs and audiologists have available and still require and the types of intervention/treatment systems that are being implemented in the schools for learners with special education needs (LSEN) in KwaZulu Natal.

## METHODOLOGY

### Research Aims

#### *Main Aim*

The main aim of the study was to describe the perceptions of SLPs and audiologists regarding their services in schools for LSEN in KZN.

#### *Sub Aims*

a) To describe the demographical information of the SLPs and audiologists in the KZN province. Focusing specifically on; the district the professional is employed in, the predominate disability the school caters for, the years of working experience in special schools and the participants highest qualification
b) To describe the caseload that the SLP and audiologists
c) To explore the resources available to the SLPs and audiologists

A survey design was implemented that incorporated closed and open ended questions. A self-administered questionnaire was sent via email out to 36 participants who met the criteria for the study. 13 of which were SLPs, 10 audiologists and 13 dual qualified SLPs and audiologists in schools for LSEN in the KZN province. Convenient purposive sampling was used to recruit the three Speech Language Pathologists (SLPs) and five dual qualified SLPs and audiologists. To be included in the study all the participants were required have a minimum of an Honours Degree in Speech Language Pathology and/or Audiology and be registered with the Health Professionals Council of South Africa (HPCSA).

A pilot study was conducted to determine the feasibility of the questionnaire. Two dual qualified SLPs and audiologists working in a school for LSEN were recruited to participate. The results of the pilot study showed that the terminology used was sufficiently clear for the participants and that the questions yielded responses that were able to address the objectives of the study.

### *Instrument Used*

The questions were developed and guided to the sub aims of the study. The questionnaire comprised of 5 sections (demographics, caseload information, resources, intervention and skill development).

## Procedure

Ethical approval was obtained from the University of the Witwatersrand Human Research Ethics Committee (Non-medical) prior to the commencement of the research (protocol number H100 305) (Appendix D). Approval from the relevant department of education and schools was also sought before mailing out the questionnaires.

Reliability for the current study was ensured by implementing inter-rater reliability measures. This involved the analysis of a quarter of all questionnaires by a second party. Member checking can be used to enhance validity and trustworthiness (Bailey, 2007). This was used as a follow-up method to validate and verify responses, i.e. the researcher contacted participants telephonically or via email when analysing the questionnaires to clarify the responses.

# RESULTS

Results were analysed by using thematic content and will be presented according to stated aims of the study.

## a) Demographic Information

The following demographic information was obtained (See Table 1).

**Table 1. Summary of demographic information of participants**

| Participant | School | Predominant disability at the school | District employed in | Years of experience | Highest Qualification |
|---|---|---|---|---|---|
| 1 | A | Physical disability and medical syndromes | Umlazi | 12 | Bachelors degree |
| 2 | B | Intellectual impairment | Umlazi | 3 | Bachelors degree |
| 3 | C | Cerebral palsy, Autism and Learning Disability | Pinetown | 20 | Bachelors degree |
| 4 | C | Cerebral palsy, Autism and Learning Disability | Pinetown | 14 | Bachelors degree |
| 5 | C | Cerebral palsy, Autism and Learning Disability | Pinetown | 20 | Bachelors degree |
| 6 | C | Cerebral palsy, Autism and Learning Disability | Pinetown | 5 | Bachelors degree |
| 7 | C | Cerebral palsy, Autism and Learning Disability | Pinetown | 4 | Bachelors degree |
| 8 | D | Deafness and hard of hearing | Pinetown | 4 | Bachelors degree |

As seen from the above table all participants have a bachelors degree as there highest level of qualification. The years of experience working in a special school range from a minimum 3 to a maximum of 20 years. The 8 participants work at 4 different schools. 75% of the participants are employed in the Pinetown district and 25% of the participants from the Umlazi district.

## b) To Describe the Caseload That the SLP and Audiologists

The SLTs and Audiologist were asked to describe their caseload in terms of the disorders they service at their respective schools.

**Table 2. Description of disorders on Caseload**

| Type of disorder | Responses |
|---|---|
| *Speech and language* | *Total 44* |
| Preschool | *7(15%)* |
| School age | *8(18%)* |
| Neurogenic | *6(14%)* |
| Dysphagia | *4(9%)* |
| Fluency 3 | *3(6%)* |
| AAC 5 | *5(11%)* |
| Early Intervention | *2(4%)* |
| Articulation/phonology | *4(9%)* |
| Hearing Impairment | *3(6%)* |
| *Audio* | *Total 14* |
| Basic Audio | *6(42%)* |
| Behavioral Site of Lesion | *1(7%)* |
| Otoscopic Immittance | *5(36%)* |
| Hearing Aid Evaluations | *1(7%)* |
| Hearing AID Orientation | *1(7%)* |

As depicted in Table: 2 there was more speech and language intervention being conducted than audiological services in the schools. School and preschool age language disorders (34%), were the most prevalent disorders on the Speech and language therapists' caseload followed by neurogenic and dysphagia(23%). Regarding audiological services 42% of responses performed basic audiometry, and 36% did otoscopic emittance.

### *Workload*

When the therapists at the four schools were asked if they were coping with the numbers of students on the caseload, three out of the four schools indicated that they needed more speech therapists and audiologists. The other school which employed five dual qualified therapists indicated that were coping and did not need additional help.

### *Referral for Therapy Services*

Respondents reported that the students on their caseloads came from various referral sources.

Regarding within school referrals 79% (11/14 ) responses stated that their sources of referrals were teachers, team screenings and assessments, and classroom observations. 21% (3/14) responses indicated that their referrals were from outside the schools such as clinic, hospitals and other therapists.

## c) To Explore the Resources Available to the Slps and Audiologists

### *Resource Allocation*

Five out of the seven respondents indicated that there were not allocated a formal budget. The funds that they needed were obtained through fund raising and private donations. One of the participants who worked as an audiologist stated that she was allocated a budget that was sufficient to meet her all equipment needs. One respondent indicated that she did not have a budget and was in desperate need of up to date equipment. Regarding the equipment needs respondents who were providing audiological services, (5/8) reported that had the basic audiological equipment and only one respondent had adequate hearing aid equipment. Regarding speech and language equipment 88% (7/8) respondents indicated that they had standardized speech and language tests but they were outdated and they needed more current up to date tests. One responded stated they needed more culturally appropriate tests, another reported they needed tests that were more appropriate for the cognitively impaired child and they also required FM systems to be installed in the school.

## d) To Determine the Continual Educational/Professional Development Needs of the Therapists

### *Continuing Education*

Regarding CPD all participants indicated that they attended workshops. Two out of the eight respondents were self funded, five partially funded by the school and one fully funded by school. Regarding further training **55%** (10/18) of the responses indicated that they wanted further speech training especially in the areas of autism, Neuro- Developmental Training, Dysphagia, Augmentative and Alternative Communication. 45% (8/10) of the responses wanted further training in audio especially in area of Central Auditory Processing Disorders, aural rehabilitation, FM systems and OAEs.

# Discussion

The results will be discussed as per four sub aims of the study. The study set out to determine the perceptions regarding the role of the SLP and audiologist in schools for LSEN, specifically the demographical status of SLPs and audiologists, the availability of SLPs and audiologists, the caseload of the SLPs and audiologists, resources that the SLPs and audiologists had available and the types of intervention/treatment systems that are being implemented.

## Demographic Information

The participants were employed at four different schools, i.e. School A for the physically handicapped (1 dual SLP and audiologist), School B for the severely mentally handicapped (1 SLP), School C for the neurologically impaired and cerebral palsied (2 SLPs and 3 dual qualified SLPs and audiologists) and School D for the Deaf and hard of hearing (1 dual qualified SLP and audiologist). From the info provided by participants it is evident that the schools are still operating in the traditional framework of Special ed schools. That is special needs school catering for a specific disability. This is in direct contradiction to the WP6 which states that schools are to serve as resource centres, serving a variety of disabilities. However, it is encouraging to note that schools for LSEN were specialised to deal with specific communication disorders. This indicates that the DoE in KZN is aligning itself with White Paper 6 (2001), which makes it clear that schools for LSEN will be strengthened by improving its resources, teachers and therapists to deal with the disabilities that present in the schools.

The years of working experience of the participants varied from a minimum of 3 to a maximum of 20 years. The length of experience and level of competence of the participants within their specific fields of practice ie; SLT or A was also varied. The implications of this is that those participants who had been working within the special education setting for a longer period of time are more experienced, have more knowledge and expertise to provide specialised intervention and treatment for LSEN. South Africa is a relative newcomer to inclusive education and can benefit from the theoretical journeys and practical experiences of those professionals that have had many years of working experience within the school sector for LSEN (Walton et al., 2009).

## Caseload-Description

All participants provided mostly school age language intervention. This is to be expected as therapy is provided within a school context for these learners. Together with specialised speech and language intervention within the school it is the SLPs role to; explain the role that language plays in curriculum, assessment, and instruction, as a basis for appropriate program design, explaining the interconnection between spoken and written language, identifying and analyzing existing literature on scientifically based literacy assessment and intervention approaches, assisting in the selection of screening measures, helping to identify systemic patterns of student need with respect to language skills, assisting in the selection of scientifically based literacy intervention, planning for and conduct professional development on the language basis of literacy and learning and interpreting a school's progress in meeting the intervention needs of its students (ASHA, 2006).

In terms of audiological services offered, all participants (except Participant 2) provide basic audiometric testing but no special testing like ABRs and CAP testing. Pure tone evaluation which is crucial aspect of basic audiometric testing is the most fundamental measure of hearing (Harrell, 2002). ABR is an electrophysiological recording of the electrical activity of the $8^{th}$ Cranial Nerve and auditory brainstem in response to auditory stimuli (Don and Kwong, 2002). Furthermore the ABR tests neural synchrony, i.e. the ability of the CNS to respond to auditory stimulation in a synchronous manner. All participant's except Participant 8 that was employed in a Deaf School reports not fitting hearing aids. The implications of this are that learners have to fit hearing aids privately or within public sector.

Interesting a study was conducted by Lesser and Hassip (2006), in Newcastle United States of America (USA) that looked at three types of professionals who were potential referrers to the speech therapy service were questioned about their knowledge and opinions of speech therapy. The answers showed that teachers were the least well informed about many aspects of speech therapy; including the nature and location of the work and the range of disorders for which such therapy is available (Lesser and Hassip, 2006). It was thus recommended that teachers should cooperate with other professionals in working with those children with special needs who are now being educated in mainstream schools, there would seem to be a strong need for teacher training to include more information about speech therapy. These findings are in negation to the current study, as all participants stated that they get constant referrals from teachers and support from teachers regarding their role in the school.

## Workload

It was noted the four therapists that worked in one urban school (previously privileged) reported that the posts available at their school are sufficient to meet the needs of the school. However, this does not accurately portray the lack of SLPs and audiologists in the KZN province. It should also be noted that this response was only from one school that participated in the study and excludes the other 20 schools that do not have speech therapy and audiology services.

DOE (2001), states that children in schools for LSEN have the right to speech therapy and audiology services should they have learning difficulties, communication limitations as well as hearing difficulties. In a study by Khoza-Shangase and Masoka (2009), it was found that there is a generalised need for more posts to be filled within special schools in Gauteng. There is a high demand for speech and language services to deal with large numbers of learners in special schools. These results have a direct implication on the KZN province where the population is the highest in South Africa and thus the need for support in special schools is even higher.

It is of utmost importance to highlight the fact that schools for LSEN within the Pinetown district are previously advantaged schools from historically "white" areas. Thus these schools are well resourced. Schools for LSEN within the Umlazi district are previously disadvantaged schools from historically "black" areas. This suggests that there is still a divide between rural and urban and furthermore previously disadvantaged and advantaged schools.

63% of the participants reported being able to cope with the number of learners receiving speech therapy and/or audiological services. When these results were compared to a similar study done in Gauteng at schools for LSEN it was found that over half (55%)of the therapists reported not being able to cope with the numbers of learners receiving speech therapy and audiological services, with a clear indication that more therapists are required in 69% of the schools. The majority of the participants (63%) are from the same school and contradictorily also stated that 23 learners are in need of therapy but are not receiving it. Participants 1, 2 and 8 felt that they required more SLPs and audiologists. This supports the issue of skill shortage of SLPs and audiologists in KZN in the schools for LSEN setting.

## Referral Sources

Participant's reported receiving their caseload from a variety of sources. Majority (79%) of referrals to SLPs and audiologists caseloads came from within schools. The participants reported that their referrals sources within the schools included teachers, team assessments, SLPs' class observations and screenings. From the latter an assumption can be made that collaboration was occurring between SLPs and the other professionals in the schools. Collaboration includes assisting general education classroom teachers with universal screening, participating in the development and implementation of progress monitoring systems and the analysis of student outcomes, serving as members of intervention assistance teams, utilizing their expertise in language, its disorders, and treatment (DOE 2001). Teachers and other professional's awareness of speech therapy and audiological services offered appeared to be well established, based on the fact that the majority of referrals were 'in-house'.

A small percentage (21%) of the referrals were from outside school sources, namely, hospitals, clinics and other therapists. This is supports the recommendations from the WP6 which stipulate that schools LSEN are to serve as resources centres for learners with disabilities.

# Resource Allocation

Majority of the participants do not have a budget for acquiring therapeutic materials and audiologic equipment. There is a lack of policy guiding the procurement of the necessary resources to support learners with disabilities. This coupled with lack of funding earmarked for intervention materials and technology seems to suggest that although the South African government has introduced major education reforms and adopted an inclusive education policy, ensuring that learners with communication difficulties and other disabilities access quality learning remains at the margins of government transformation initiatives.

There seems to be no political will that ensures that funding for learners with disabilities is made available. It appears that most provincial departments of education do not view issues relating to children with disabilities as a priority. It would appear that provincial department is prioritizing HIV/Aids programs.

The lacking of government funding in contravention to the statement made by the UN Convention (2008) which states that full inclusion guarantees the right of every child to attend a regular school with the support they require, thus emphasising the goal for full inclusion in regular education systems. This research highlights the importance having a funding policy in place if the UN convetion and White paper 6 is to be fully implemented.

According Cater, Lees, Muria, Gona, Neville and Newton (2005), there is an increasing demand for culturally appropriate assessment tools for speech, language and hearing disabilities developing countries.

Due to the nature of cultural variation and the potential for cultural bias, new assessment tools need to be developed or existing tools require adaptation. However, there are few guidelines on how to develop 'culturally appropriate' assessment tools (Cater et al., 2005).

It has been established in South Africa that the majority of clinicians assess and treat children from a culture different to their own (Cater et al., 2005). Awareness of cultural variation, bias and cooperative efforts to develop and administer culturally appropriate assessment tools are the foundation of effective, valid treatment programmes (Cater et al., 2005).

The fact that one participant cited that she was in need of impairment specific material (for learners with intellectual disability) is a barrier to providing holistic functional therapeutic intervention.

There has been a shift from viewing disability from a medical approach towards an ecosystemic (bio-social) approach. This approach undergirds the recommendations that have been put forward by the WP6 that states that special schools need to begin shifting from organizing services according to disability categories and move towards the level and nature of support needed by the learner (Landsberg, 2008).

It can be suggested that this type of approach can be used to overcome the issues in terms of resources that the participants are faced with. By assessing the learners not only using formal assessment measures but also a variety of other resources such as observations, parent reviews, family interviews which are core aspects of the ecosystemic approach.

## To Determine the Continual Educational/Professional Development Needs of the Therapists

### *Continuing Professional Development (CPD)*

CPD refers to any activities aimed at enhancing the knowledge and skills of therapists, teachers and other professionals by means of orientation, training and support (Lessing and de Witt, 2007).

All participants conveyed that they attend CPD workshops and activities. Furthermore attending workshops enhances ones personal and professional growth by broadening knowledge, skills and positive attitudes (Lessing and de Witt, 2007).

It was evident that all the participants felt that they required specialised training pertaining to the area of disability they were working in. Limited specialised knowledge in a specific disorder may hinder the effectiveness of treatment. Identifiable variables that the participants reported on included; resources available, caseload dilemmas, support and training needs. Participants also indicated that they have good systems in place in terms of notification on courses, workshops and activities taking place.

## Limitations

The results of this study are likely to be somewhat bias due to the sample size in that only 8 out of 36 SLPs, audiologists and/or dual qualified SLPs and audiologists participated in the study. Therefore, one is not sure if those who did not participate would have responded to the questions differently. However, the researcher would like to believe that the few participants that answered the questions were honest regarding their role in schools for LSEN. Although it is difficult to ascertain this, the study provides a small indication of the role of a SLP and audiologist in schools for LSEN in KZN.

The response rate to the questionnaires was low and this was the risk of a self-administered questionnaire research design.

Babbie (2009), states that a low response rate is a danger signal, because the non-respondents are likely to differ from the respondents in ways other than just their willingness to participate in the survey.

## Implications

Despite the limitations of the study the results highlighted the need for more intensified efforts in to improving speech therapy and audiology services within special education schools. Prioritizing services to children with special needs should be on the agenda of the Department of Education in South Africa with regards to the establishment of post structures that can be filled appropriately utilised to meet the needs of the learner. Furthermore, incentives need to be put in place to retain and recruit therapists who are committed to providing speech, language and audiology services.

The further build on the data that was collected for this research, the following are implications for future research;

- The study be replicated to larger sample size and using a different method of data collection, to fully ascertain the current role of SLPs and audiologists throughout the entire KZN province
- A comparative study to be done to compare the results of the current study with that of a similar study conducted in Gauteng by Khoza-Shangase and Masoka (2009).
- The study be replicated across all the provinces in South Africa to gain a national awareness and status of the role of SLPs and audiologist within the schools for LSEN setting.

# Conclusion

Findings suggest that there is a lack of SLPs and audiologists in the rural and urban districts in KZN, with more SLPs and audiologists in the urban sector. Due to the lack of posts available for speech pathologists and audiologists not all learners are receiving speech therapy and audiological services even though they are entitled to. Furthermore, the majority of SLPs and audiologists reported that were not coping with their caseloads. However, despite not coping with the numbers of learners needing services; referral sources and support from principals and teachers appeared to be well established. Regarding resources and availability of clinical materials; formal assessments needed to be culturally relevant. Concerning CPD activities and workshops the participants reported on attending them on a regular basis.

Given the complexities and challenges highlighted in the study it is not always possible to predict with certainty how the above implications will impact the interaction between relevant stakeholders and systems in the education sector in South Africa.

## REFERENCES


American Speech-Language and Hearing Association (ASHA), (2006). Responsiveness to Intervention: N*ew Roles for Speech-Language Pathologists.*

Carter, J.A., Lees, J.A., Murio, J.M., Gona, J., Neville, B.E.R. and Newton, C.R.J.C. (2005). Issues in the development of cross-cultural assessment of speech and language for children. *International Journal of Communication Disorders.* 40 (4), 385-401.

Department of Education (2001), White Paper 6. Special Needs Education: Building on inclusive education and training system. *Pretoria: Department of Education.*

Department of Education (2002), *Draft guidelines for the implementation of inclusive education* (2nd draft). Pretoria: Department of Education.

Edgar, L.D and Rosa-Lugo L.I. (2007). The Critical Shortage of Speech-Language Pathologists in the Public School Setting: Features of the Work Environment That Affect Recruitment and Retention. *Journal of Speech and Hearing Services in Schools.* Vol.38 31-46. Orlando: University of Central Florida.

Khoza-Shangase, K. and Masoka, N. (2009). *Speech Therapy and Audiology Services in Special Schools in Gauteng, South Africa: The current status.* Un-published report for the Gauteng Department of Education (GDE).

Landsberg, E., (2008). *Learning support.* In Landsberg, E., Kruger, D., and Nel, N. (Eds.). *Addressing barriers to learning: A South African Perspective.* Pretoria: Van Schaik Publishers.

Lesser, R. and Hassip, S. (2006). Knowledge and opinions of speech therapy in teacher, doctors and nurses. *Child, care, health and development.* 12 (4), 235-249.

Lessing, A. and de Witt, M. (2007). The value of continuous professional development: teachers' perceptions. *South African Journal of Education.* 21 (1), 53-67.

Prevalence of Disability in South Africa: Census 2001. *Statistics South Africa.* Pretoria: Statistics SA.

Statistics South Africa. Census 2001. *Prevalence of disability in South Africa.* Pretoria: South Africa.

Walton, E., Nel, N., Hugo, A., and Muller, H. (2009). The extent and practice of inclusion in the independent schools in South Africa. *South African Journal of Education.* 29; 105-126.

# INDEX

## B



## C

## D

## E

## F



## G



## H



## I

## J



## K



## L



## M

## N



## O



## P

## Q



## R

## S

## T

## U



## V



## W



## Y



## Z